Katy & Linda –

Wishing you Successful
Communication!

Sarita
Alderson, Chapter 7

THE PRODUCTIVITY PATH

Your Roadmap For Improving Employee Performance!

DAVE ARNOTT • TRACY BROWN • SHERRY BUFFINGTON • PEGGY COLLINS
CHANDLER GEORGE • JP MARONEY • SARITA MAYBIN • REBECCA S. MORGAN
BETTE PRICE • GARY RIFKIN • MARK SADLEK • PAULINE SHIRLEY
LINDA BYARS SWINDLING • RUSS YAQUINTO

MaroCom Publishing Company
A division of JPMaroney International

For information contact:
MaroCom Publishing Company
c/o JP Maroney International
PO Box 9492
Tyler, Texas 75711-9492
1-800-304-5758
www.JPMaroney.com.

Learn about other titles in The Path Series at www.PathSeries.com

FIRST EDITION

Cataloging-in-Publication Data
Maroney, JP, 1970 –
   The Productivity Path : Your Roadmap For Improving Employee
Performance / JP Maroney, editor
   p. cm. (The Path Series)

ISBN: 0-9704592-0-3

   1. Personnel Management
I. Title.   II. Title: Your Roadmap For Improving Employee Performance

HF5549.P75
658.3–dc21

INTRODUCTION

When I pulled together the thirteen co-authors who joined me in writing this book, I commissioned them with one objective; answer the question so often asked by employers...

"How can I improve the performance and productivity of my employees?"

The result is a book which contains fourteen distinct, yet complimentary perspectives on the topic of improving employee performance in the workplace.

You will find a number of ideas, suggestion, techniques and principles within the pages of this book. I suggest you select one or two ideas you believe will work in your organization, and then try them. Put them into action, and see if they work for you.

If you want to go further, we've included contact information for each co-author on the first page of their chapter. Each co-author is a recognized expert in their field, and most provide additional services like: professional speaking, training, and consulting.

At the back of the book, you'll also find listings of other resources available from co-authors including: books, audio and video programs, assessment tools, and employee training systems.

I hope you find this book enlightening, inspiring, and highly useful in your quest to bring out the best in your people.

Best of Success,

JP Maroney

Co-Author & Publisher

PS: Look for other titles in *The Path Series* at www.PathSeries.com

TABLE OF CONTENTS

TABLE OF CONTENTS

CHAPTER ONE

When There Isn't A Fight – Start One!

How Leaders Can Build Commitment in Corporations, Schools, Sports Teams and Families.

Dave Arnott, Ph.D.

Dave Arnott is a professional author, speaker, consultant, and educator. He holds a Ph.D. in Management, and teaches in the College of Business at Dallas Baptist University where he was named professor of the Year in 1999.

Dr. Arnott has appeared as an expert analyst on the CBS program 48 Hours, and is regularly quoted by regional and national media regarding organizational and sports management issues.

Dr. Arnott is author of *Corporate Cults: The Insidious Lure of the All-Consuming Organization* (AMACOM Press, 2000), named "best business book of the the month" and nominated for book of the year.

Employee Development Seminars:
- Project Management
- Executive Leadership
- Work-Life Balance

Keynote Topics:
- Corporate Cults: When What I Do Replaces Who I Am
- Persistence: The Greatest Predictor of Success
- When There Isn't A Fight: Start One

The Arnott Organization
Rowlett, TX • (972) 475-7164 • www.davearnott.com

Dave Arnott, Ph.D.

When There Isn't A Fight – Start One!

How Leaders Can Build Commitment in Corporations, Schools, Sports Teams and Families.

"When there isn't a fight, we start one!" said Southwest Airlines Vice President Colleen Barrett. At first, I thought she was crazy. Hadn't I taught my students and seminar attendees just the opposite, to put OUT fires? Conflict is bad, not good. Unless you think in economic terms. Economics is the study of the distribution of scarce resources. An assumption of economics is that you can't create nor destroy goods, you simply move them around.

That's the assumption Ms. Barrett was making, which I now understand and agree with: a certain amount of conflict will always exist, and it's the leader's job to put it where he/she wants it. Identification of an external threat rouses and consolidates the troops to fight against a common foe. External pressure produces internal cohesion.

Based on this assumption, the leader's job is not to "Put out fires," but to "Start them." They start fires outside the organization to cause the group inside to coalesce.

The shell that separates the organization from its environment is semi-permeable. When conflict is settled with outside forces, the conflict doesn't go away, it simply seeps inside the organization through its membrane. Thus the objective of leaders is to continually find or create outside threats to eliminate internal conflict. When viewed as an economic good, conflict will always exist. So the leader's job is not to squelch it but to simply move it around.

The economic concept of conflict can be seen in many different types of organizations; from schools to the military, from sports to politics. All groups maintain some level of competition with their external environment. The leader's ability to identify and focus attention on an external threat increases the level of organizational commitment within the organization.

"When There Isn't a Fight, Start One!" is a thought-provoking idea that will change how you lead and manage your organization. It will help you concentrate your energies to produce greater employee commitment and goal accomplishment. That's because employees of companies in the new millennium use the same tribal commitment-building techniques to fight off environmental threats that were used by the cavemen centuries ago. The need for organizational commitment and the presence of external threats has not changed over millennia. The techniques for producing it haven't changed either. External pressure still creates internal cohesion.

External Pressure Produces Internal Cohesion

War Veterans are drawn together by more than loyalty to their country. They also have a loyalty to each other that was born of surviving a difficult situation together. The same is true of shipwreck and airplane crash survivors, and Super Bowl and Stanley Cup champions. You can also put in that group employees who survive downsizing, restructuring, lay-offs, labor strikes, mergers and acquisitions, bad bosses and tough sales quotas.

Everyone who has worked together in a group has survived external pressure, which has created internal cohesion for their group. The greater the external threat, the greater the internal cohesion.

The internal cohesion necessary for organizational commitment cannot be obtained without external pressure. Conflict is a natural part of any organization. By "starting a fight" the leader is not creating anything that didn't already exist, he/she is simply following the laws of nature.

The Nature of Conflict in Corporations

Leaders know there is conflict in their organization, but they often don't understand why. It's because conflict is a normal part of everyday life. Trying to eliminate conflict is unnatural.

Conflict exists in fiefdoms throughout all organizations. It's natural for mid-level managers to desire ownership of the work their group is performing. With ownership comes pride in quality, performance and goal completion. When fiefdom ownership expands, it overlaps with other fiefdoms and conflicts emerge. THIS IS GOOD!

The only way to avoid these fiefdom conflicts is for managers to take less pride in their work. By taking pride, and thus accepting ownership of their work, these natural conflicts will emerge. Managing them is the leader's job. The first step toward conflict management is to understand that the leader's job is not to extinguish, but only to manage conflict. It's explained via the concept of social economics.

Social Economics in Organizations

Economics is the study of the distribution of scarce resources. The money I have in my pocket when the day begins may very likely be somewhere else at the end of the day. I haven't created nor destroyed the money, I've just moved it around. I'm the father of two teen-agers, so when I don't move it efficiently enough, they help me.

The concept of social economics is exemplified via time, the most fixed and scarce of all resources. You can't create nor destroy time, you can only use it. The same is true of organizational conflict: you can't create nor destroy it, but the adept leader can use it to increase organizational commitment.

Instead of coming to the office dreading the conflict you'll have to deal with, you should be rejoicing because it means at least two good things are happening: 1. Mid-level managers are accepting ownership and pride in their work which is spilling into the fiefdoms of others, and 2. You have a great deal of conflict energy to direct the way you want it to go.

Let's say Tom and Nancy are having a conflict. You call both of them into your office under the guise of a planning session. Then you have a confederate of yours walk by the office and make casual comments (which you can all hear) about how lousy the entire department's performance has been. "The whole department sucks!" your actor friend states loudly. Tom and Nancy are likely to look at each other, exclaim "No we don't!" and you've won the battle because you've got the former combatants using the plural pronoun "we."

The next section reminds you of how pronouns changed from singular to plural in response to external pressures in your family.

Siblings and Corporate Brotherhood

You and your siblings would probably fight like cats and dogs until the neighborhood bully came around. Then, the family would close ranks to protect one another. The same dynamic probably happened in your workplace today. The natural tendency to produce conflict is only changed by a larger threat that effects both siblings - or departments in the business scenario.

If your mother understood and used the "external pressure causes internal cohesion model," she wouldn't spend her valuable time trying to settle fights among you. She would be creating fights outside your family circle. As a leader, you should do the same: Don't make peace, create war.....with a pre-described enemy.

The result of external pressure is internal cohesion. A book I authored in 2000 explains how corporations use this external pressure to create internal cohesion via cult leader techniques to create Corporate Cults.

Corporate Cults

Corporate Cults describes the ten techniques used by traditional cult leaders which use external pressure to create internal cohesion. Since authoring the book, I've visited many organizations where I've helped them identify and strengthen the positive elements of their organizational culture and de-emphasize the negative elements.

Often, organizational leaders are too close to their organizational culture to see how their actions reinforce negativism in their employees. I help them by contributing an objective point of view and a framework for analyzing their culture and aligning it with their organization's strategic plan to achieve better results. That often involves identifying the appropriate times to adapt the idea, "When there isn't a fight, start one!"

Do you think your organization is not very cultish? Your high school probably used external pressure to create internal cohesion.

The School Myth

In preparation for a speech to the National High School Coaches Association, I conducted a small survey of high school athletes, coaches and administrators by asking the simple question, "Why do we have high school sports?" The answers from administrators were the most surprising, "To perpetuate the school myth," one of them answered.

I understood the idea of mascot, school colors, school song, identity, and belonging, but I was taken back by how overt the principal was about the manufactured nature of school spirit. She went on to explain that students need something to identify with. If they buy into the school myth, they become owners of the school identity and defend it against attacks. If they don't buy into the myth, they drift away and attach to an identity outside the school, which could include negative influences.

The principal's assumption was correct: It's human nature to want to belong to something. Less than 3% of high school dropouts are involved in extracurricular activities. The effect is that "owning" the school myth keeps teenagers attached to their high school.

The school myth couldn't exist without competing against other school myths. The natural "my school is better than your school" is encouraged by the school myth. "Good" is a relative term. A particular school can't be "good" unless it finds one that is somehow less than good.

The school myth is perpetuated by high school administrators as a means of using external pressure to create internal cohesion. It's also used to create cohesion in one of the most loyal organizations in America, the mafia.

An Offer you Can't Refuse: Building Commitment the Mafia Way

The mafia is perhaps the best example of an organization that draws distinct lines between members and non-members. There are definite in-groups and out-groups in mafia life. Everyone in the family is protected, no one outside the family is protected.

Integrity is when you integrate what you say with what you do. By that definition, the mafia has the highest integrity of any organization I know. When they promise to break someone's legs, they do it. When they pledge loyalty to the family, they keep their pledge. Sammy the Bull Gravano is a big news story for breaking out of the mob because he's a huge exception to the norm.

The mafia builds commitment by declaring clearly that external pressure creates internal cohesion. "When there isn't a fight, they start one" to create internal cohesion. It works in sports teams as well.

Sports & Competition

When an opposing coach or a newspaper writer makes negative comments about her team, the coach doesn't dismiss the comments as simply part of the game. She posts the comments on the team bulletin board because she's very accustomed to the idea that "When there isn't a fight, start one!"

This is often used to bring a fractured team back together. Nothing cures team infighting more effectively than identifying a common external foe. This works particularly well with athletes, because they're accustomed to the idea of conflict that contains winning and losing. So when athletes get into business or other organizational situations, they automatically think in terms of win-lose: Who's on my team and who's on the opposing team? Because athletes are trained to become team members, they're very accustomed to the idea, "when there isn't a fight, start one!"

Politics & Power

Politics is the "fruit fly" of this concept. Fruit flies are used in genetic research because their fast reproduction produces multiple generations very quickly. Politicians re-group into coalitions on a daily – sometimes hourly – basis. They will join with one group on a particular issue, and simultaneously belong to another group that contains a whole different set of members.

There is no other social entity in which in-groups and out-groups change members with such speed and regularity. The nature of a representative democracy demands the making of "strange bedfellows." The political arena is a good case study for "When there isn't a fight, start one," because there are multiple fights in politics that take place simultaneously.

There are political formations in all organizations. While they may not form and reform as quickly as they do in true politics, they still exist. You will do well to recognize the formations of these political groups in your organization, which will lead you to an understanding of how the cyclical formation of interest groups in the political arena is very similar to group formations in your organization.

To Gain Pleasure or Avoid Pain

People are motivated by two things: To gain pleasure or avoid pain. Books, seminars, and motivational literature are replete with frameworks that accentuate the first, but ignore the second.

Goal setting, teamwork, communications and negotiation frameworks are all built on the assumption that people are motivated to gain pleasure. While that assumption is true, and it works, it's only half the equation. The pleasure framework concentrates on group goal achievement and the satisfaction that will be produced by "winning."

The gaining pleasure paradigm completely overlooks the "avoiding pain" motivation that can and should be used to motivate organizational members. "When there isn't a fight, start one!" logically recognizes the threat to group cohesion when there is no external conflict. By discovering and accentuating this external threat, organizational leaders increase external pressure, which creates internal cohesion.

Practice What You Preach

Does Southwest Airlines practice what they preach? As Ms. Barrett was sharing her dicta with me, "When there isn't a fight, start one," her airline was running a full-page ad in USA Today purposely starting a fight with their competitors and the Federal Aviation Administration. The ad featured a drawing of seven airliners - representing the seven major airlines - all wearing robber masks. The ad asserted that the seven big airlines had colluded with the FAA in changing the structure used to bill the airlines for their services.

The previous system billed the airlines for each mile flown. That gave commuter airlines like Southwest a cost advantage, because they fly shorter routes. However, it's a mis-application of the expenses incurred by the FAA, because they incur great expenses getting the airplane off the ground and back on the ground, and very little expense while in flight. Thus, a more reasonable fee schedule is to bill the airlines for each take-off and landing. That would shift the cost burden from the long-haul carriers to the commuters. While this is a reasonable reallocation of the costs, Southwest didn't miss the opportunity to "start a fight" with their collective competitors and the FAA.

The external fight created internal cohesion. Southwest CEO Herb Kelleher wrote a newspaper column that extolled Southwest as the scrappy underdog who was being unfairly treated by the bigger airlines. This external pressure – whether real or created – caused internal cohesion and commitment among the troops.

Choose Your Fights Carefully

The advice "when there isn't a fight, start one!" comes with a rather serious warning. Fights must be chosen carefully. Often a fight will continue and escalate for a long time period. So the external combatant must be one with whom the organization can afford to maintain a adversarial relationship for an extended period of time.

Maintaining the balance between the two sources of motivation: gaining pleasure and avoiding pain, is a delicate matter, and you should not attempt to generalize from one organization to another. A careful study of organizational culture is the best way to determine the correct balance of these two very different motivational techniques. "When there isn't a fight, start one!" can produce very positive strategic goal accomplishments when applied carefully and accurately.

CHAPTER TWO

Improving Employee Productivity in a Multicultural Environment

How to maximize productivity by managing diversity.

Tracy Brown

Tracy Brown is President of Person To Person Consulting, a human resources consulting and training firm based in Dallas, Texas. She is the author of the book, *"Breaking the Barrier of Bias"* and four audio programs, including: *"motiVersity™: Motivating While Valuing Diversity"*.

Tracy has designed or delivered diversity training for clients like American Heart Association, The Sabre Group, Dallas Central Appraisal District, American Express and the FAA.

At Parkland Health & Hospital System, the YWCA and City of Dallas, she's conducted customer service training. And when Sky Chefs, Mrs. Bairds Bakeries, and Kaiser Permanente needed external support for Human Resources projects, they called on Person To Person Consulting.

Areas of Expertise:
- Diversity Strategy
- Cross Cultural Communication Skills
- Teambuilding
- Assessing and Building Team Trust
- Excellence and Empowerment

Person To Person Consulting
Dallas, TX • (888) 316-4447 • www.TracyBrown.com

Tracy Brown

Increasing Employee Productivity in a Multicultural Environment

How to maximize productivity by managing diversity.

Take a deep breath. Clear your head. Now respond to the following questions with the first word or phrase that comes to mind.

"What is diversity?"

"What does it mean to manage diversity?"

"What does diversity have to do with productivity?"

When I hear the word "diversity" the corresponding phrase that comes to my mind is "differences of all kinds" or "variety." When I see the phrase "managing diversity" the immediate thought which surfaces for me is "maximizing productivity."

But when most people see or hear the word diversity they think "discrimination." And many people define "managing diversity" as "avoiding discrimination" or as "eliminating or punishing racist and sexist behavior."

It is easy to understand why people focus in on the problems associated with diversity. What often gets the most attention are sensational court cases, extreme violations of civil rights and political issues which divide us. We don't often see the examples of people from different cultures sharing together, resolving conflict or learning from each other. We have much less exposure to examples of organizations, issues and experiences where people with different cultural norms or experiences see those differences as a distinct part of their strategic advantage and use those differences to expand their capabilities.

Diversity Impacts Productivity

In the workplace 'valuing diversity' and 'managing diversity' are both about maximizing productivity. And diversity refers to many more characteristics than simply race, ethnicity and gender!

Think about it this way. Each employee has a limited amount of time and energy to perform the required tasks and to complete the assigned work. Completing that work includes building relationships and effectively communicating with others.

How much potentially productive time is wasted when employees are fearful of being excluded or judged negatively by coworkers and others? In your work environment:

How might an employee who is gay be regarded if he placed a photograph of his partner and himself on his desk?

How might a file clerk with a hearing impairment be included in staff meetings and informal gatherings?

How might a person for whom English is a second language be treated when coworkers form teams in order to complete a work assignment?

What attention is typically given to dietary requirements based on religious or cultural norms of non-Christian (or non-meat-eating) employees when planning a departmental luncheon or a company activity involving food?

When is the last time you participated in a group discussion where elements of diversity were being discussed as a way to improve communication, develop innovative solutions or increase revenue?

Would you want to work in an environment where you were judged based on who you are, rather than on the work you do? Would you want to work in an environment where you felt others did not value you, or worse, where coworkers excluded you, because they were uncomfortable with your name, your accent, the location of your home or the religion you believed in? Of course not!

And most of us wouldn't want to be found guilty of making our coworkers feel excluded unfairly or our customers feel disrespected. Most of us avoid the obvious behaviors that cause discomfort. We know what is illegal. We don't tell racist jokes. We downplay gender stereotypes.

But race and gender are only two of the elements which arise in any serious discussion of diversity. There are many factors that make each of us different from one another. And most of us are not equipped to see those differences as positive catalysts for stimulating growth, creativity, education and energy in our teams at work.

Instead we've been socialized to "stick with our own kind" and to focus on the ways we are alike. We have been shown the deficiencies in people who are different from us then warned to avoid "those people" and the things they represent.

We are taught that the territory called differences is filled with land mines which will explode and have the effect of killing relationships. So instead of learning to deal with inevitable misunderstandings in a mutually serving way most of us instead choose to avoid the field completely. We stay with people like ourselves or with people who make us comfortable.

We subscribe to the uncomfortable insincerity of being 'politically correct' instead of engaging in thoughtful and authentic conversation where there is room for mutual learning and mutual growth. And we look for behavior and information that supports our assumptions so we can feel justified excluding and judging others using our own experiences as the measure of what is right or successful.

Individual Behavior Influences Productivity

These things all affect our productivity when we enter the workplace where there are colleagues and customers who are different from us. It then becomes our choice whether to make diversity a barrier or a positive contributor to success.

In a best-case scenario, employees who feel excluded or unfairly judged spend a lot of time making others comfortable, hiding their differences or feeling devalued. In a worst-case scenario these same employees spend time sabotaging team results, rebelling against unfair treatment, spoiling the company's reputation in the community or fighting back through lawsuits or negative media coverage. This time and energy could be exchanged for more productive activities.

Employees who are part of the "included" and "valued" groups also suffer. They miss out on the opportunity to expand their knowledge, participate in creative problem-solving and prepare for the continued changes which result as our society becomes more global and more driven by technology.

Finally, the entire company suffers if customers who represent a wide variety of cultures and norms feel misunderstood or ignored. They become more likely to switch to a competitor who makes them feel understood and valued or who anticipates their needs in new ways.

Building Trust

Most would agree that trust is a key ingredient in building or maintaining a productive work environment. When people who are very different from each other work together the relationship often begins in an environment where there is very little trust. We don't trust this person who is different from ourselves and we don't trust ourselves to be effective with this person we don't know.

Often employees will say, "I just don't trust that person." But when questioned further, the lack of trust has nothing to do with anything that specific employee has done or said. More often than not the capacity for trust to exist is based on our own experiences in the past with others who the employee reminds us of. This is especially likely if the person not trusted represents a cultural group we are not familiar with or a group that is associated with many negative stereotypes.

Is it any wonder that black employees often don't trust white employees? Or men don't trust women? Or younger workers don't trust older workers?

In an environment where diversity is part of the strategic advantage, employees are less likely to interact with each other based on stereotypes and assumptions. This results in a higher level of trust. Employees who feel they are trusted by others to do the right thing in a wide variety of situations are more likely to be productive team players who provide excellent customer service.

Self Assessment

Most of us are very quick to make statements like, "I'm not prejudiced." or "I'm comfortable with diversity." It is easy for us to claim innocence or profess enlightenment then point out the deficiencies or mistakes of others. But if you really want to make a positive difference and help diversity become a positive part of productivity in your company then I suggest you start by increasing your self-awareness.

Try this. For the next 24 hours pay attention to the subtle messages in your environment that reinforce the importance of being alike – or emphasize the danger or discomfort of being different.

The easiest target for review is marketing. You might recognize patterns in television commercials and in advertising in magazines and newspapers that suggest what people who are fun, successful, smart, efficient, wealthy, responsible or beautiful might look like.

Conversely, you might notice what people who are untrustworthy, undependable, unsuccessful, unattractive or undesirable look like.

But don't stop there. Look for the subtle signs in your neighborhood and wherever you work. Who is most likely to be comfortable, and who might be uncomfortable, in your environment?

And if you are really brave, don't just look outside of yourself. Walk through your home and look at the kinds of books on your shelves, the message you might be sending with the clothes you wear and the list of activities on your calendar for the next 30 days.

If you have children, think about the educational and spiritual environment you have placed them in. Consider your recent choices for family vacations and other leisure activities.

Throughout this exercise of observation, ask yourself the following questions:

- Does this show a pattern that implies one group or type is inherently better than another?
- What are the preferences this pattern indicates?
- What have I chosen not to be exposed to? What types of people do I know very little about?
- How does this affect my relationships with coworkers or customers in the work environment who don't reflect the characteristics or qualities I value?

This activity is not designed to reveal you as a person who is a closet racist, sexist or some other negative label. Instead, it will hopefully create a deeper awareness in you about subtle ways you limit yourself and unintentional ways you communicate whether others are welcome or not.

From Awareness to Action

When diversity is valued in the workplace:

- People work well together and employee retention improves or stabilizes
- Customers are served in ways which meet or exceed their expectations
- Revenue increases as a result of identifying and connecting into new markets (or by increasing market share in current markets

There are many specific things each of us can do to value diversity in ways that help to increase productivity (both our own productivity and the productivity of others).

Inquire

You can begin this immediately. Challenge yourself to ask at least one person who you consider different from yourself in some significant way a question each day. The questions you ask must be either educational or trust-building in nature.

Avoid questions that reflect your own biases or preferences. For example, "Why do Muslims pray 5 times a day?" might be a better question than "Why aren't you Christian like the rest of us?"

In addition to the new information you will learn over time, this practice supports increased productivity because it helps you become more comfortable asking questions, exploring new possibilities and expecting those who are very different from you to have valuable input. The behavior will carry over when you are problem-solving on work-related issues or tasks.

Another way this supports increased productivity is that it positions you as someone who sees each person as an individual and is respectful of all.

Selecting Teams

When selecting partners to complete an assignment, or when selecting employees to work on a team project, challenge your assumptions.

Even when we think we are choosing participants based on objective merit, we have to question ourselves. Why is it that you think the employee who graduated from a specific school is a better risk? Is the employee who makes you feel most comfortable able to challenge you and make you think? And is the person who has always gotten good performance reviews the one who will give you the most creative solutions?

Valuing diversity can help you identify benefits from partnerships that would otherwise be unlikely. Valuing diversity can support team performance that is more innovative than expected. And valuing diversity can improve customer service by bringing a variety of perspectives and experiences to the forefront when planning products, services and resolutions to customer problems.

Research

In the business world in general, many of the heroes and role models have been men who are white, Christian, heterosexual and able-bodied. But there have been many people who excelled in business who were from other groups. How many do you know and how many can you educate others about?

This kind of research is informal, but it supports increased productivity over the long-term because it broadens the image in your subconscious mind about what characteristics are required to be successful. It will also result in you seeking out ideas from people you might not have approached before.

Improving Communication

One of the most powerful things we can do to transform our awareness about diversity into positive and productive behaviors is to pay attention to our verbal and written communication.

It is simple to train yourself to speak warmly to everyone in your department and to those you pass in the hallway each day. When you speak to only specific people you can unintentionally imply that only they are worthy of your time and attention.

In both verbal and written communication we can limit our use of slang, colloquialisms and complex sentences. This makes it easier for people with different language skills and different levels of literacy to understand our message.

We can insure consistent work flow by breaking task lists and instructions into small steps. We can present those steps in the order they should be followed.

We can avoid questions which can be answered with "yes" or "no" and instead ask open-ended questions that give us answers which verify information or confirm understanding.

Building Alliances

We can build alliances that result in more creative problem solving and in acquiring a broader customer base by building positive relationships with people from different groups.

Improving Customer Service

We can anticipate customer needs by seeking input from people who represent fast-growing groups in our community or marketplace. The hospital that adds a Spanish-language channel to its television stations sends a subtle, but powerful message to its patients who speak Spanish. A manager of a retail store who visits the churches, stores and other community institutions in the area surrounding the office learns more about what customers need and expect.

Increasing Productivity in a Multicultural Environment

Almost everywhere in the United States it is apparent that the workplace is changing. Our applicants, coworkers and customers represent more cultural groups than ever before.

To be productive we must pay attention to the skills and talents needed to perform the job. We must also pay attention to the environment we create in our workplace so that we maximize productivity.

Building trust across cultural boundaries, developing communication skills that bridge cultural styles and norms and challenging ourselves to become more comfortable with difference will help us progress more quickly up the path to productivity!

CHAPTER THREE

Cultivating Exceptional Employees

Understanding and Influencing the Four Factors
that Determine Employee Outcomes

Sherry Buffington, Ph.D.

Sherry Buffington is founder and president of Peak Potentials, a training and consulting firm, and of SkillBuilders International, Inc., a publishing and product development firm. She has spent more than twenty years studying human behaviors and personalities, and applying her extensive knowledge to optimizing individual and group functioning in both personal and professional arenas.

Dr. Buffington is co-creator of the highly acclaimed C.O.R.E. Multi-dimensional Awareness Profile and author of *Who's Got the Compass?...I Think I'm Lost!* She holds a Ph.D. in the field of Psychology

Training Programs:
- Employee Effectiveness
- Management and Leadership
- Selling and Customer Relations
- Team Building
- Communications (Verbal and Non-Verbal)
- Motivation and Conflict Resolution

Peak Potentials
Dallas, TX • (214) 688-1412 • www.coremap.com

Sherry Buffington, Ph.D.

Cultivating Exceptional Employees

Understanding and Influencing the Four Factors that Determine Employee Outcomes.

If you've ever found yourself feeling more like a parent, trying to keep unruly children under control, than like the leader of intelligent adults, you're not alone. Managers nationwide report that undirected, unenthusiastic, poorly performing employees are increasing, and worry that this growing problem will destroy morale and undermine the efforts of the entire organization.

Although most companies are at a loss as to why this trend is growing, evidence suggests that, in many cases, the companies themselves, in an effort to prevent employee dissatisfaction and avoid lawsuits, are unwittingly contributing to the problem.

There are four primary factors that determine employee outcomes. These are (1) company culture, (2) employee attributes (3) management, and (4) employee attitudes. Each interacts with the others and affects them to a large degree. Ultimately, all four factors must be aligned for optimal performance. How seriously these categories are addressed and managed determines, almost entirely, how effectively an organization and its employees will function. To better understand how these four factors may be affecting your organization, let's briefly examine each of them.

Environment and Company Culture

Every company has its own particular cultural environment, which functions somewhere within the boundaries of fast-paced or slow-paced, highly structured or flexible, stressful or relaxed, employee-centered or process-centered. Even in the healthiest of cultures, there will be certain types of employees who fit better than others. It's extremely useful to know which ones fit, and how to effectively manage those who don't.

Generally a company's culture falls somewhere between healthy and mediocre, but there are two types that are decidedly unhealthy. One is a "No Mistakes" culture, in which everyone is called out on the carpet for any little mistake. This results in a fear-paralyzed workforce that doesn't dare do anything new or innovative. Companies stagnate and eventually die within this overly strict culture.

The other unhealthy culture falls at the opposite extreme. It's a "No Consequence" culture, which on the surface might seem to be a laid-back, easy-going environment. What's really going on however, is that managers have decided that problem employees require so much of their time that it's just easier to ignore them than to deal with them or find effective ways to manage them.

Unfortunately, the longer managers tolerate sub-standard work and negative behaviors, the worse they tend to become. Worse yet, other employees notice that difficult employees are "getting away with murder" and, in time, they too begin adjusting their productivity levels downward to the lowest level tolerated. Soon the majority of employees are simply riding the time-clock, collecting their paychecks, and doing just enough to stay out of serious trouble. Even potentially excellent employees function far below their capacity in such environments.

Once employees become accustomed to coasting, complacency sets in and turning the tide can be a real challenge, but it can certainly be done. There are ways to stop almost any downward spiraling trend, but any real and lasting change must begin with upper management and filter down. It is essential then, for company leaders to understand the reasons behind employee behaviors, and get serious about implementing measures that are known to develop and nurture productive, dedicated workers.

Values-based management, which uses a set of principles to guide the decisions and directives of every employee, coupled with a people-centered approach has proven to be highly effective in all kinds of organizations.

Employee Attributes

While no two people are exactly alike, all people fall into particular classifications that are useful in defining them and their abilities.
The classifications generally used in the workplace, such as gender,
age, education level, and work experience, are far less important than
the less regularly used classifications of personality type, natural
traits and abilities, behavioral style, values, emotional maturity and
character.

Many companies never bother with the latter classifications,
believing they are "soft skills" incidental to getting the job done.
Nothing could be further from the truth. Volumes of research data,
such as the broad study done by U.C. San Diego professor, Dr. Judith
Bardwick, clearly proves that character and personality influence
behaviors and outcomes on the job more than knowledge and skills.
Dr. Bardwick states, "It is much easier for an individual to learn new
skills and information than it is to change one's personality and
character; to make a timid person bold, for example."

Healthy character, one of the two components named as primary to employee success, is not possible without sufficiently developed emotional maturity, or as author Daniel Goleman coined it,
"emotional intelligence". In fact, emotional intelligence is cited in
study after study as the number one predictor of outstanding performance in the workplace.

I have been training and consulting since 1984 and have seen
more instances of well educated, experienced employees who are
also highly problematical due to emotional immaturity, than I can
count. Time and again I have found that an employee's level of emotional maturity is directly proportional to his or her overall effectiveness. Yet, few organizations address this issue.

Emotionally immature employees can wreak havoc at any level,
but the higher up the organization immaturity flows, the greater the
problems become. Emotionally immature employees are the sources
of petty politics, time-wasting gossip, loafing, slacking off, and a host
of other completely counter-productive behaviors. It is estimated
that these behaviors cost organizations more than forty billion dollars annually.

After emotional immaturity, the next greatest cause of employee
problems is trying to make employees perform well at something for

which they have no natural abilities or inclinations. It's like trying to teach a turtle to fly, but managers waste endless hours and millions of dollars essentially trying to do just that.

Poor job fit occurs when employees are placed without any consideration of their natural attributes, which is an expensive mistake. There is no way an individual can sufficiently alter natural abilities to excel at the wrong kind of work. A natural athlete, for example, with minimal technical acumen will never be an exceptional computer programmer. He may learn the basics and perform the tasks to some level of competence, but he will never shine at it. Conversely, an individual with natural technical intelligence, but minimal athletic abilities, will never be a star athlete. As in the first example, he may learn enough skills to compete, but he too will never be a star. Reverse the roles of these two, however, and each of them will quickly shine in the area of his natural talent.

The same rule applies in the workplace. It is not uncommon to see people who have little propensity for details occupying jobs such as bookkeeping, filing, data entry, editing and other positions that require attention to detail. Though they work hard at getting it right, lots of costly mistakes occur. It's also fairly common to find introverted technical or systems-oriented people, with few people skills, in customer service positions. Many customers are lost at the hands of these individuals, who likely mean well, but just don't like dealing with people (and it shows).

Another major contributor to employee problems is poor communication and understanding between managers and their employees. Managers tend to be direct, to the point types, and that's how they communicate. However, the majority of people are indirect communicators who process information differently, and who need more discussion or explanation than most managers are willing to give. They rarely ask for more information though, and often the result is directives that are carried out wrong or poorly.

Managers are frequently frustrated by the poor results and assume it's because the employees can't follow orders. Usually, however, it's because managers start at "Z" (the outcome they want) and work forward. Employees, with different temperaments, start at "A" (the first step of a process) and work forward. So while the manager is talking about "Z", the employee is at "A" trying to figure out what on earth the manager is trying to convey. The solution is often as simple as learning how each type of person communicates, and communicating to them in their way.

Communications, day-to-day interactions, outcomes and productivity all improve markedly when managers and their employees understand one another's personalities and learn to build on one another's strengths. Most people want desperately to get along with others and to do their best. They simply need the means for doing it. Before this can occur, organizations must invest in programs that ensure every employee, including managers, can recognize the differences that exist among personalities and learn how to best work together. It is also extremely important to discover each employee's natural abilities and place them where their talents are best utilized.

Management

Statistics compiled by The Small Business Administration state that nine out of ten businesses that fail, do so because of poor management. One incompetent manager can quickly destroy the morale of an entire department and, from a senior management position, of the entire organization. Where morale is lacking, so too is respect, dedication, ingenuity, forethought, productivity and just about everything else necessary to organizational success.

Great leaders are great because they are competent, not just at managing systems, but at understanding and developing their people. They have excellent people skills, which they apply wisely in order to get the most from every employee. True leadership is the ability to persuade others to do things your way and like it. To get that result, one must know what will persuade each individual and what will make doing the job enjoyable.

Without good people skills, the role of management will always be a challenge. I have asked hundreds of managers to name the source of their greatest challenge and ninety-nine percent of them name employees. The challenge can become far easier, and even enjoyable, when approached from a position of human awareness, as many of my clients have discovered.

One client, concerned about an employee he had promoted to management eight months earlier, confided that this individual, who had been an excellent employee for seventeen years, had suddenly become angry and tyrannical as a manager. He couldn't understand it. A profile of this employee revealed that, while she enjoyed working with people, she was not comfortable in a leadership role. But, wanting to please her manager, she was giving the new position all she had in spite of the extreme stress it was creating for her. The negative behaviors were a manifestation of her high stress levels.

My client didn't want to lose this valued employee so, upon my recommendation, gave her the option of moving back to her old position without taking a pay cut, provided she assist whoever replaced her as manager. The employee happily accepted the offer. She soon returned to her old, kind, reliable self and, three years later, is still a valued employee. Had my client not worked with this employee's nature and needs, he would have eventually lost her.

After learning about human nature and how it impacts behaviors and interactions, numerous managers have told me, in hindsight, that they too have lost valuable employees by promoting them to positions for which they were unsuited or by unknowingly mismanaging them. They also frequently marvel at how profoundly the combination of culture, individual attributes, and management impact employee performance and attitudes.

Employee Attitudes

In 1993 I was called into a large organization which, two years earlier, had implemented a program designed to unify employees and management. However, instead of improving morale and productivity as intended, things had steadily declined. Employees were sullen and cranky, and petty wars were raging everywhere. The first thing I did was conduct confidential interviews and really listen to what the employees had to say. Essentially, what they told me was that they had been collectively wounded by the uncaring attitudes and lack of concern that had existed at all levels of management for years. Many of them had voiced their concerns about this and management's answer had been this "joke of a program". Nothing, the employees asserted, had changed except that they (the employees) were now supposed to pretend that everything was all better.

The managers were quick to point out that the company had spent a quarter of a million dollars on this program, telling the employees they should be grateful. But they weren't grateful. They were furious! And their furor was driving their attitudes and behaviors. The employees knew their productivity had decreased and their behaviors worsened. They didn't care. They wanted to be seen, heard and acknowledged, in a genuine way and they had no intentions of making any improvements until that occurred.

Unfortunately for this company and its employees, top management was too immature and self-absorbed to hear what the employees were clearly conveying. They refused to make the suggested changes. Ultimately, the brightest, most employable people left to work elsewhere. The job turnover rate in this organization is still extremely high and productivity low. The problem continues to exist because a vicious cycle has developed and only the healthy intervention of top management can stop it. That won't occur until someone healthy (and emotionally mature) moves into that position.

The cycle likely began with a company culture that was too process-oriented. The employees, feeling overlooked and unappreciated, began complaining to their managers, who felt powerless to change the culture and so responded with what appeared to be indifference. This caused the employees to develop an indifference toward the company and its goals, which led managers to feel the need to tighten controls. This further alienated the employees, and the cycle just kept getting more vicious.

Looking at this scenario, it's easy to see how all four factors are out of sync. Anytime you see a general malaise and wide-spread poor attitudes among employees, you can bet this is what's happening. But attitude alone can set off a similar outcome on a smaller scale. When, for instance, one department is dysfunctional, it might be because the manager of that department is dysfunctional or perhaps there is a problem employee with a bad attitude keeping everyone else stirred up and off-balance. Like one bad apple, one bad attitude can spoil the whole bunch given enough time and latitude.

Because the causes of employee problems can be broad and varied and each factor plays on the others, the exact cause may at first be hard to see. But, whatever the cause, the good news is, it's curable. But it must be cured at its source, and the source is people.

New systems, re-engineering, quality circles, team-building exercises, incentives, raises, and all the other things commonly tried, will be temporary fixes at best, unless the source of the problem is addressed and healed. Healing comes from understanding.

Understanding brings cooperation and cooperation fosters good working relationships. Good working relationships produce results, better results improve productivity, and greater productivity increases profits. The path to real and lasting productivity and profits will always be that of cultivating exceptional employees. Invest in it, and you'll discover it's a path of many great returns.

CHAPTER FOUR

The Science of Networking

How to put the "Magical" Art of Connection to work in Your Organization

Peggy Collins

Peggy Collins has guided thousands of individuals, entrepreneurs, managers and sales teams to "break through" the connection barriers.

From Top Real Estate Producer to Senior Vice President of a banking institution to President of Peggy Collins Enterprises, Peggy applies 30 years in sales and marketing to electrify and ignite your people.

Peggy propels people into action. She connects with her audiences immediately and motivates them to act. The professional in networking know-how, Peggy models successful people connections. Peggy teaches you how to connect... with your co-workers, supervisors, associates, and new contacts!

Presentation Topics:
- Market Yourself Successfully – Inside and Out
- Sales is Not for Sissies
- How to Overcome the Common Cold Call
- A Woman's Place is in the Heart
- DE-Stress Your Distress: 21 Days to a New You

Peggy Collins Enterprises
Dallas, TX • (972) 233-3175 • www.thepeopleconnector.com

Peggy Collins

The Science of Networking

How to put the "Magical" Art of Connection to work in Your Organization.

The "Power of Connections" is magical! I demonstrate this magic in keynotes and workshops all over the country. "Who would like to see the magical power that I feel in this room right now?" I ask an association audience. Almost every hand goes up. I have previously chosen three names that are well known, depending on the city that I am in. In Dallas, it would be the Mayor, a Dallas Cowboy and George W. Bush. "There are people in this room that can network to George W. in three calls or less. Would you please stand up." In a group of 25-50, there will be 3 or 4 who will stand. "How about a Dallas Cowboy?" There will be 7-10 that will stand. Then, I really open it up-"stand if you know a CEO, an interior designer, a landscape architect, an information systems manager, an accountant. Large groups of individuals stand with each one. The energy in the room is escalated. The magic begins to infuse this group. They begin to understand.

A Harvard study done in 1967 reveals that each of these people knows, on average, between 500 to 1000 people. If we take the low number of 500, with 25 participants, we have 12,500 potential connections represented, and since we have no idea who people know, the "magic" begins.

Every day, these same people in my audience are part of a corporation, organization or firm where there are individuals who radiate this same magical power - the power to connect us beyond our present database of friends, associates, suppliers, and customers. All the information, referrals, advice, mentoring, resources, job changes/career changes, or new employees are within our grasp. Are you effectively networking and connecting?

Let me take you on an exciting journey through this process. It has befriended me through the years as my all-time greatest life-skill. It has brought me much business, and beyond that, it has brought meaningfulness to my life as I have connected and repaid the favors.

If you are a manager or a leader in an organization, are you and your organization networking to your full potential? We have gone beyond the transaction economy and we are now doing business in the "Relationship Age". Teams, partnerships and alliances are the "buzzwords" of the day.

You can tell it's the Relationship Age, I'm sure, from looking at the Internet and the mirroring of relationship-building principles. Amazon.com says, "Hi, Peggy, glad you are back. We have some recommendations for you." Start noticing the commercials on TV. Count the number of times that the words "connection", "relationship" and "trust" are used. Maybe your organization is using these words in advertising materials. Wayne Baker in his book Networking Smart says, "In the new business world, networking smart - making connections and building relationships - is the key to personal and organizational success."

What are the networking principles to master that will insure your employee's and your organization's success? Let's take a look.

The Science of Networking - Principles

Credibility and Trust:

Why do we need networking at all? Why not just call someone and ask him or her for the information that we need? Credibility! We need to borrow the trust that exists between two people so that the targeted individual will feel comfortable to be open with us.

"The more trust there is, the easier it is to do business. As trust accumulates - in teams, corporations, communities, and nations - it creates a new form of wealth. ....'social capital' is as potent a source of wealth as land, resources, skills, and technology", say Jessica and Jeffrey Stamps in their book, The Age of the Network.

Rapport:

Successful relationship building requires the skill to build rapport. Rapport is the good French word that means harmoniousness. We most often build rapport through looking for commonality. What do we have in common? Same schools, same friends, same old neighborhood, fraternity or sorority?

A number of years ago, I worked with Dick Valentine, an advertising executive from Chicago. He attended a party for a new employee at his twin brother's advertising firm. The brothers and the new employee, Bill, started to chat. They soon discovered that they were all from Chicago - from the same area - from the same street, even from the same house. Bill's family had purchased the home from the twin's family. Over the years, as a child, Bill had played with an army jacket he had found in the attic. Over the pocket was the twin's last name, Valentine. Now, that is commonality!

After we have established rapport with someone, we look for common interests, values and goals and it is through these deeper commonalties that strong relationships grow - the art of connection in living color!

"A People-Care" Attitude:

The effective networker is an individual who sincerely cares for others. What if we came to work each day, focusing on how we could help each of our workmates become more successful? What human resources could we pass along to make this happen? Who would be the winner?

I recently jumped into a cab at the Los Angeles International Airport on my way to a conference. As I engaged the driver in conversation, I learned that he had owned a French restaurant that had gone bankrupt. In despair, he thought about suicide, he said. One of his friends had suggested he drive a cab to get out of his apartment. "What that did was give me back my life. People are good and they want to help." One of his creations in the restaurant had been a wonderful sauce and one of his passengers was helping him market it.

Caring relationships make "pay-back" an integral part of networking. Some are reluctant to network, feeling that they are using others, until you point out that this is a reciprocal agreement.

Listening

Listening for the needs of our network is a great way to reciprocate. Christmas shopping last year, I stopped to buy a piece of luggage at a shop that has been around our neighborhood for years. It was apparent that they had diversified-gifts and food products. Just as I approached the counter with my purchase, a customer asked the lady at the cash register, "Do you all carry truffles?".

"No, I'm sorry, we don't," she answered.

Jumping into the conversation, I told the customer that I had a good friend, a fellow member of The National Speakers Association, Kali Schnieders, who had just written a wonderful book called *Truffles From Heaven*. A candy company was packaging their chocolate truffles with the book. The customer was delighted. She contacted Kali and a huge purchase of books and truffles resulted. What fun! It's about listening for the needs of those in our networks.

Foundations:

In networking terms, the database of all of our connections becomes our foundation. It is from these relationships that our credibility, our rapport is utilized in the myriad of strategic ways I listed at the beginning. In order to network systematically and strategically, we are constantly expanding this base. What will benefit you personally and professionally? Which organizations would be beneficial to join? What suppliers could keep you posted on developments in the market? What financial analysts could advise you of impending changes in the industry? What groups peripheral to your industry or profession would expand your "circles of influence"?

It has been proven that the more diverse your network is, the wider your reach will be! I have seen this played out so wonderfully in the Six Degrees of Kevin Bacon Game. In the game, one person names a movie star. The other's challenge is to tie Kevin Bacon to that star in 6 connections (stars) or less through movies that they have each appeared in.

The reason this is so effective is that unlike some stars, Bacon's movie career has been so diverse, such diverse roles, that he has appeared with a wide variety of stars, allowing him to be linked easily to others.

So it is with us. If we have a wide variety of interests, children who are in activities, a mate that has a job in a totally different industry, participate in organizations, belong to a sports club, and attend the theatre, then before you know it, we are a "Kevin Bacon" and become the "hub" of a huge network. In so doing, we have gained the ability to help ourselves and everyone inside our networks as well.

Informational Interviews:

Information has become the "collateral" for success. Learning organizations grow and change based on it. Internally or externally, an information-gathering base is a powerful tool. An informational interview is an effective method for getting information, advice, support, asking for referrals, or brain-storming,

When you identify the individual with the expertise you need, utilize a member of your network to network you to the expert. Call, mentioning the name of the referrer: "Sally suggested that I call. She says that you are an expert when it comes to team building. I wonder if I could buy you breakfast and pick your brain"? At the interview, the last question should always be "what can I do to help you"?

Informational interviews can be extremely helpful for:
1. Learning how your position fits in to the overall strategy of the organization
2. Gaining advice
3. Networking more deeply to experts
4. Seeking a Mentor
5. Problem solving/brainstorming
6. Locating partnerships/alliances
7. Finding new suppliers
8. Team-based projects requiring information gathering
9. Word-of-mouth marketing

Easy As 1-2-3

More often than not, we achieve our goals at the 3rd level out from our own network, which is our foundation. Networking challenge: We need a new supplier, someone who will set up an Intranet within our organization. Going to our foundation base, we have lots of people who are in the technology area, even one who is a LAN (Local Area Network) Administrator. He is the one we decide to call. He gives us two referrals to possible firms. These represent our 2nd level. Another person (2nd level) in our network recommends one of the same companies the very next day, so we call that firm. This represents our third level out. See how it works?

Networking Your Organization?

What changes can you put into place as a leader that will benefit employees individually and the organization as a whole?

1. Hold classes to give your employees an in-depth knowledge of the Principles of Networking, applying them to your particular vision, strategy and mission.

2. Set up signage "Look Out, Networking Ahead" to keep people ever mindful of a new commitment for a networked organization.

3. Create a Mentoring Program for all levels. Ask each Mentor that signs up for the Program to agree to meet with his/her mentee on a regular basis and ask for evaluations at benchmarks along the way.

4. Organize activities that mix people cross-functionally. This will create problem-solving opportunities. Some companies design new office space to create cross-functional traffic patterns that will enhance these opportunities.

5. Set up a lunch or coffee break area and name it the "Network Nook" to create awareness.

6. Add networking to your performance appraisal and make suggestions for improvement. Help your employees grow.

7. Network across your organization to gain the support of all the management. Look at all the network building you can do along the way!

8. Set up a company-wide Networking Breakfast. Ask each of your fellow managers to invite a customer, supplier, partner etc. Have a specific topic for each meeting that will help all of you grow professionally. Go to that breakfast with specific networking goals in mind.

9. Establish awards for community and association involvement.

10. Don't forget the Internet. Use the same Principles to gain access to experts in your particular field. It is an amazing phenomenon that needs to be experienced as experts and authorities are only a click away.

The Payoffs:

1. Higher employee morale/ team spirit
2. Better retention because of built-in support systems
3. Cross-functional brainstorming and problem solving
4. Word-of-mouth marketing
5. Marketing yourself
6. A sense of pride and involvement in the company as a whole
7. A feeling of connection and belonging
8. Targeted team projects outside the company
9. Better customer retention because of resource sharing
10. Locating better resources and suppliers through outside networking
11. Recruitment of better employees
12. Employees managing own careers
13. Finding partners/alliances
14. Industry-wide information gathering
15. Tracking competitors

After my presentation was over to the association, I stood talking with some of the participants who had come up to share.

"I wish you had asked if anyone knew someone in the Whitehouse. I worked there for two years."

"Peggy, I found my job across the country from where I was presently employed, and it happened at the fifth level out. You're right, people do want to help."

"I don't know what would have happened when I became ill last year if I had not had my network. My family was thousands of miles away. I always thought of my network as a business network, but they brought meals, took me to the doctor, and raised my morale."

The magic is there! It is in the faces of the people, the meaningfulness that comes from connecting, and the success that happens when we apply it to our personal and business lives.

Your goals are within your reach; won't you reach out?

CHAPTER FIVE

Ageless Energy in the Workplace

How to turn negative stress into positive energy, and improve employee performance and productivity.

Chandler George, D.C.

In his 11 years of chiropractic practice, Dr. Chandler George has personally treated more than 7,000 individuals to wellness through cutting-edge technology and passionate caring. As a wellness expert, Dr. George has developed a unique approach to educating patients about total wellness concerns, in additional to the traditional chiropractic approach.

Dr. George was team physician for the U.S. World Masters Power-Lifting Championships in Budapest, Hungary. As a top motivational speaker, Dr. George ignites audiences with his enthusiastic, effervescing energy to love themselves, get healthy and "e-mail stress to another planet!"

Audiences Learn How To:
- Feel young and vibrant, regardless of age
- Never have to "call in sick" again
- Be laser-focused and productive all day
- Stay calm and confident - even in stressful situations
- Reduce or eliminate aches and pains - without medication
- Enjoy peaceful sleep, and energized mornings

Dr. Chandler George
Weatherford, TX • (817) 599-0061 • www.drgeorgedc.com

Chandler George, D.C.

Ageless Energy in the Workplace

How to turn negative stress into positive energy, and improve employee performance and productivity.

We all suffer stress; it's a part of the American way of life. Now, stress has invaded the workplace. Today, employees are no longer doing "three Martini lunches," but rather eating and working at the same time. The average work week is now up to 47 hours - 4 hours more than two decades ago. "Workaholism" is a new disease whose primary symptom is STRESS!

Has "twenty-four/seven" become a new formula in the American business community due to the new technologies we've been handed? Are we actually on call 24 hours a day, 7 days a week? This brings up the questions: Are we overworked? Are these changes in our lives good for us?" The general consensus is these technologies are improving society; but there's a catch - the more we become connected, the more detached we become from the more human elements of life.

What happened to fun and enjoyment - what happened to taking time to smell the roses, or enjoy a sunset, or listen to the happy laughter of a child?

Reducing stress, and improve performance and productivity can be as simple as making sure that each employee gets breaks and lunch times; that each employee feels the appreciation of the employer; and, better still, that each employee is evaluated frequently to ascertain his/her level of performance.

Look at the whole picture - maybe an employee is not happy doing a certain job; look at his/her talents and potential - just maybe you want to do some shifting of personnel to ensure that each employee is satisfied and working to his/her full potential.

The warning signs

"I couldn't sleep at all last night." The first line of the 1958 song, "Tossin' and Turnin'" by Bobby Freeman, and one of the greatest laments among people of all walks of life. Ever lose sleep over a problem? Why? Stress and worry seem to be major occurrences in life. Your employees Got stress? Got worry? Here are the early warning signals:

Whiner and/or winer

This includes the "poor little me, no one understands me" syndrome. A "whiner" is an unhappy person and needs serious attention. Then there's the "winer" (sound the same, but different problem). This person thinks a few drinks will solve all problems and help him/her to forget. That works temporarily, but then he/she wakes up from the effects of the alcohol and is in worse depression than before the binge.

Complainer and blamer

This person finds fault with everyone else, and someone else is always to blame for what happens. This person is never at fault.

Cynicist

This person is always making unkind remarks about the success of others, or the condition of the world; just can't find anything right with the world. Isn't that a shame?

Tylenoler

This is a weak person's remedy for "can't get a good night's sleep." Using a drug to sleep may be fine, until the next day when the person needs to be sharp; the aftereffects may inhibit his/her ability.

Helping your people help themselves

Know your employees; work with them to convert the negative energy of stress to a positive energy. That way, instead of going to sleep with problems, they go to sleep with peace and a clear mind, and wake up with a solution, have a positive attitude and feel good about themselves and their jobs.

Three little words to help are "write everything down." Keep a pad and pen beside the bed. Write down what needs to be done the next day and prioritize that list from the most important to the least important. Then, even if the list isn't finished the next day, the most important items have been handled. Having your employees work in this fashion relieves a great amount of stress and thereby increases productivity and performance. Many CEO's have paid huge amounts of money just to have this information imparted by "efficiency experts."

Remind your employees, when they get under the covers, to think of past successes or good times; carefree times - vacations, friends, past victories, and all that for which they are grateful. If an occasional "brain sparkle" occurs in the night, it should be written down. Unload everything! When the conscious mind is clear, it provides unobstructed channels from the subconscious for solutions and new ideas, and provides undisturbed sleep. Choosing this method provides mental freedom which creates opportunities not available to a cluttered mind. This makes the employee "sharper" the next day, adding to his/her performance and productivity.

Recognizing Energy Draining Personalities

We are all human and all fraught with the same frailties, and any employer should recognize these distortions in his/her employees:

The "All or Nothing" Thinker - This person sees only black or white; there are no variations, no shades of gray.

The "Overgeneralizer" - This person views negative events as a never-ending pattern of defeat and can't figure out how to overcome the defeats;

The "Mental Filterer" - This person dwells on negatives

The "Positives Negator" - This person firmly believes his/her positive qualities/accomplishments don't count;

The "Mind Reader" - This person assumes, with no positive evidence, that people will react negatively;

The "Fortune Teller - This person predicts, arbitrarily, things will turn out badly;

The "Magnifier or Minimizer"- This person either blows everything out of proportion, or reduces its importance;

The "Emotional Reasoner" - This person assumes himself/herself to be an idiot because he/she feels like one;

The "Personalizer/Blamer" - This person blames him/herself for something for which he/she is not entirely responsible, or blames other people and denies his/her role in the problem.

These are areas where the employer must know the employee, must be aware of his/her negativisms and react with the appropriate suggestions and help.

Your body's STRESS "Auto Pilot"

The body actually has an automatic mechanism, like a reflex, to allow each of us to cope with stress. This is termed the "fight or flight response" and it sends the body into high gear to confront or escape from a threat. The body releases two hormones (Ephedrine and Norepinephrine) into the blood stream that equip the body to handle emergency situations. Heart rate, breathing, alertness and muscle response increase and this reaction to stress creates overload - a eventual health hazard.

Attitude is crucial in stress management. Teach your employees to: "Believe in yourself, your values, your choices and your decisions. Most of all, remember that you control the influence over the course of your life; focus on self-improvement and regain that control. "

Stress is part of the struggle - a natural occurrence in the drive for success. But stress and worry are individual choices; a mind has thoughts which either show up as stress and worry, or the mind harnesses the same energy and converts the thoughts into resolve.

"Stress Triggers" and "Stress Inhibitors":

Stress Triggers:

Caffeine	Sugar	Tobacco
Salt	Overeating	Refined Carbohydrates
Alcohol	Medication (Tranquilizers)	

Stress Inhibitors:

Proper Diet	Exercise	Chiropractic Care
Meditation	Massage	Breathing
Sleep	Positive Mental Attitude	

Tips for Ageless Energy in the Workplace

Be aware of when your body and mind need reenergizing. Give yourself permission to take a break.

Build breaks into your schedule. You need breaks every one-and-a-half to two hours.

Disengage and really relax. Take a walk or use other relaxation techniques to sever your mind from work and create your own oasis of calm.

When planning long meetings, don't forget "brain sparklers". Use fast breaks to increase team energy and focus.

Heed the "breaking point." At 3 o'clock, take 15 minutes, have an apple, and do a diaphragmatic breathing exercise.

Do a sleep audit. If you're not sleeping well, change your habits and monitor the results.

Plan adventurous vacations....And take them.

Shun one-dimensionality. Constant work leads to dullness and/or burnout. Cultivate relationships and outside interests to foster energy and balance.

Energize Your Life!

Balance Eating Habits! A thumbnail of good fat (canola or flaxseed oil) with every meal.

Carbs vs. Protein! 1:1 ratio at each meal; more carbs to relax; more protein to stay sharp.

Boost Your Heart Rate ! Get heart rate up to 50% of maximum once a day, five to seven days a week.

Target heart rate - take 220 minus age, then 50% of that.

Repair Nerves! Take vitamins/minerals (especially B6, B12, Vitamin C and E). Consult doctor before starting any program.

Set G.O.A.L.S! Great Obstacles Appear Less Scary with goals. Set small goals, go step-by-step, then celebrate when achieved and reset for a new goal. Goals are the passion of life. They are the get up in Get up & Go!

Desire vs Fear! Picture a 10" x 4" thick board across a floor that 100' long with $1000 at the end. Would you cross it? Now, picture the same board across two buildings in Chicago, would you still cross it? Now, instead of money, your child is at the other end, would you cross it? POINT - what motivates you, desire or fear?

Brain Sparklers! Try to do something in 5 minutes or less that breaks you out of your mental rut; for example, jog around the house, play with the dog, etc.

Rejoice in Life! Wake up early and walk in the neighborhood before going to work. Smell the smells, listen to the world waking up. Rejoice to be alive!

Tele-energy Booster! To increase energy, call a friend to whom you haven't spoken in over a month. Be focused on that person. There, didn't that feel good?

Positive Association! Find like-minded people who will support you, and you them, in similar activities. Good peer pressure can give you energy and momentum.

Eat for Energy! Eat 6 to 8 small meals a day to keep blood sugar levels even and energy consistent.

Plan Your Work-Outs! Plan your work-outs 4 months at a time, complete with how much to lift, when to rest, how far to run, and how long it took. Be as detailed as you can. Put it in a prominent place at home, like on the bathroom mirror.

Minimize Your Medications! Take as little medication as possible.

This will give you back energy (check with your doctor). Medications such as Paxil or Zoloft slow down your nervous system.

Music That Moves You! Find music with a beat that gets you moving. If you're moving, you have energy.

Smile! Hey, we all need one so smile and give one away now! You'll get many more in happy return!

Stretch! So easy, but often ignored! After walking, to warm up, spend 15 minutes on the floor so hips are anchored. Without bouncing, stretch hamstrings, hips, and calves (the largest muscles).

Stimulating Activities! Do a sporting or cultural activity with a friend or friends. The friendship and the activity can be very stimulating.

Breathe in Energy! Breathe deeply a few times, then hold for 15 seconds, then exhale forcefully. Begin again, easily this time. It will relax and focus you as well as give you the needed oxygen for energy.

Tune in to Good Health! Get in tune with your body. It pays to look to the cause for wellness.

Get Outside! Studies suggest that listening to water falls (gurgling water) makes us feel better. Being under a tree in the summer gives us shade and oxygen. The fresh outside air, especially after a rain, is a wonderful "pick me up" to feel more alive!

Plan Your Vacations! List your vacations for the next year. None? Then plan some, even if only to the lake for a weekend, or maybe to grandma's house out in the country. See what you've been missing!

Invent Your Day/Year! Write down ideas for the perfect day, such as fun, exercise - physical, mental, spiritual - friends, a movie, whatever! Have fun with it and then do it when you've got it. Then brainstorm the perfect year!

Avoid "Toxic" Foods! Identify foods that create a "toxic havoc" on your body and don't eat them. Note which foods increase your energy and give you a general good feeling. Keep a list of energy foods!

Doctor of the Future! "Remember the doctor of the future will give no medicine, but will interest his patients in diet, the human frame, exercise, and as to the cause and prevention of disease." Thomas Alva Edison

Have a Ball! Use a flex ball to lay on and take stress off your back. Flex balls can be found at sporting goods stores.

Drink Plenty of Water! At least half of your body weight in ounces per day!

See a Chiropractor! They are specialists in adjusting the spine, thereby making your nervous system happy!!!!!

A two-way street

This is a two-way street and must be a combined effort of management and employees. Since stress is the number one inhibitor of performance and productivity, the employer must find the best methods to eliminate it from the workplace, as well as helping his employees eliminate it from their lives.

CHAPTER SIX

Morale Builders...Morale Busters!

*How to increase employee performance
by improving job satisfaction.*

JP Maroney

"The business executive's worst fear is that their people won't care as much as they do about the organization's success," says JP Maroney. As a business strategist, author and professional speaker, JP helps organizations leverage their human capital by creating entrepreneurial corporate cultures where people at every level think and act like owners. "Most employees will never go out and start their own company, but given the opportunity, tools, and motivation they will treat the organization as if it is their own," says Maroney.

JP Maroney's strategies include:
- How to lead a mission-guided organization
- How to get people to "buy-in" to your vision
- How to improve employee morale and reduce turnover
- How to foster creativity and innovation within people
- 5 master keys to building great teams
- How to remove barriers to speed and agility
- How to implement change without killing morale
- How to create a customer-focused corporate culture
- How to foster an entrepreneurial spirit in people

JP Maroney International
Tyler, TX • 1-800-304-5758 • www.JPMaroney.com

JP Maroney

Morale Builders...Morale Busters!

*How to increase employee performance
by improving job satisfaction levels.*

Today's employee expects more than just money from their career. They seek a sense of identity, achievement, and satisfaction. As a result, companies wishing to build workplace morale and boost employee productivity should seek ways to improve employee satisfaction in the workplace. Employee satisfaction levels can be dramatically improved by hiring the right people, casting them in the right roles, involving them in the organization's improvement process, and rewarding employee achievements.

HIRE THE RIGHT PEOPLE

The "warm body" approach to hiring doesn't work anymore (as if it ever did). Today's competitive marketplace and tight labor pool, forces companies to focus on hiring the right people; people who will "fit" into the organization's culture. Three key factors in determining whether or not a prospective hire will fit into the organization include: personality, values and flexibility.

Personality

The personality of the people hired should match the company's personality. If the new hire prefers a formal, "corporate" organization, and the company has an entrepreneurial, "family" environment, the employee will feel out of place immediately. Today, some companies are creating "relaxed" workplaces with basketball courts, pool tables, and on-site massage therapists. These employers encourage people to spend more time on the job, and don't mind if workers show up in blue jean shorts and tank tops. That's their culture. And if it works for them, it's OK. But, imagine how out of place a new hire might feel if they are accustomed to marble tile, double breasted suits, and eight hour workdays. Shock therapy!!!

Part of the interview process should be to tour the company, explain the culture, let the prospective employee see other employees. Then, look for reactions and comments from the potential employee. Listen for subtle comments that provide insight into whether or not they will be happy in the organization.

Values

A potential employee's personal values should align with the company's values. Their ideas about growth, customer service, productivity, and profitability should match the organization's strategy. For example: a new "hot shot" salesperson will create conflict if they see more value in going quickly for "the close," when the company is known for building long-term relationships as solution providers. While it's not vital that employees all think alike, it is important their underlying values align with the organization's mission and purpose.

Flexibility

In today's rapidly changing business environment, an organization needs people who can be satisfied and thrive in a workplace that is constantly changing. If the organization is growing fast and constantly evolving, each employee must be flexible and open to change. If an employee is resistant to change, working for the organization will be a very dissatisfying experience, and their dissatisfaction will stifle performance.

It is important to hire with the future in mind, and think beyond the existing need. Consider the organization's growth and evolution when making hiring decisions, and look for people who can evolve with the organization. Michael Dell, Chairman and CEO of Dell Computer Corporation said it best when he wrote in his book *Direct from DELL* (Harper Collins, 1999, with Catherine Fredman), "We're not bringing them (employees) in to do a job; we're inviting them to join the company." If the organization is growing and changing, look for people who are flexible enough to change with the times while maintaining high productivity levels.

CAST PEOPLE IN THE RIGHT ROLES

One of the biggest employee morale busters is placing people in positions they don't enjoy, or where they don't have the talent, knowledge or skill to excel. When people are good at their job, they enjoy it more. And, when they enjoy their job more, they are more productive. I often say, "Love what you do, and do what you love." That includes making sure people are doing what they do best. Five tips for insuring that people are in roles which maximize their natural talents include: digging deep, examining the past, profiling their strengths, not trying to fix people, and regularly reviewing "job fit."

Dig Deep

During the interview process, asking key questions will help identify the prospective employee's strengths. Dig deep. For example, don't settle for the, "I love working with people" line as an indicator that they will succeed in the customer service call center. Instead, ask questions like, "What do you feel is your greatest strength?" Then, don't stop there. Ask, "Why?" Get the person talking, and listen for subtle messages which provide insight into their true strengths.

Examine the Past

A great way to gain insight into a person's strengths is to ask about their past successes. Ask what they have excelled at in the past. Find out what they enjoyed, and why they enjoyed it. Chances are great that what brought satisfaction and success in the past will do the same in the future.

Sometimes a person's favorite roles have been outside their careers. Inquire about club or organization memberships. For example, when looking for a new team leader, department manager, or supervisor, ask the prospective employee if they have ever served as an officer in a community organization. Ask what they liked about it, and if they enjoyed organizing events, keeping people on track, meeting deadlines, and delegating tasks to committee members. It might be wise to take it a step further by asking for the names of a couple of fellow club members who might share a perspective on the prospective employee's strengths as a leader.

Profile Their Strengths

Develop a profile of the prospective employee's strengths. In addition to the verbal interview, consider using assessment and profiling tools which help compare the person's strengths with the talents and skills needed for the available position.

It might be determined that the person is better suited for another role in the organization. It's entirely possible a new position may need to be created in the organization which maximizes the person's unique potential. That's OK, if they can add value to the organization.

Stop Trying to "FIX" People

Some employers fall into the trap of placing people in roles thinking the employee will "grow into it." These employers assume that enough training and on-the-job experience will help the employee perform at a level of excellence. Rather than focusing on, and building on the employees strengths, they send employees to seminars and workshops intending to improve or compensate for weaknesses. This is a backward approach.

Research reveals that most human behavioral patterns are set early in life. Each person has areas where they excel, and areas where they struggle. The challenge for business leaders is not to "fix" the areas where people struggle. It is to discover their strengths and build on those strengths. Focusing on the weaknesses demoralizes and frustrates the employee, making them feel inadequate, when it's possible the employee might excel if placed in a role that capitalizes on their strengths.

Ongoing Review

Sometimes a person is cast in the right role when they are hired, but over time they get promoted or shifted to a new role which conflicts with their natural talents. This "miss-casting" can be avoided by regularly discussing whether or not the employee and the role still

match. Some questions to ask include:
- What do you like about your current position?
- What would you like to change or improve?
- Where do you feel you add the most value?
- What tools, training or resources would help you maximize your full potential in our organization?

Perhaps, it sounds too simple, but it is that simple. If organizations want sustained performance and productivity, employees must be happy in their roles. Again, for employees to be happy, they should be doing what they enjoy, and what they do best.

INVOLVE PEOPLE IN THE IMPROVEMENT PROCESS

Involving people in the organization's improvement process provides one of the most powerful tools for improving employee satisfaction. Most employees, at one time or another, go home and tell their spouse or a friend, "If we would just _____, we could save the company money." Or, "If we could _____, our customers would be more satisfied, and would buy from us again." Yet, because there is no system in place, those ideas are never captured, never considered, and never used.

One of the first questions I ask organizations when I consult with them is, "What organized system do you have in place for consistently soliciting, analyzing and implementing employee suggestions for improving your organization?" Most of them just look at me with blank faces. They are not doing it. It's obvious that the leaders of these organizations either think it's too much trouble, don't know how, or just flat don't care what their employees think. I'd guess that 75-80% of the organizations where I ask that question can't give me an affirmative answer. That's sad. These companies are missing out on a terrific way to improve employee satisfaction, and also to improve the overall organization. Involving employees in the improvement process requires a system for soliciting, analyzing, and implementing ideas.

Soliciting Employee Ideas For Improvement

If an organization wants happy, satisfied employees, it must allow them to contribute ideas for improving the organization.

Why? Because people will pour their hearts and souls into something they help create. I've seen it happen in companies, in non-profit organizations, in churches, and I've seen it happen in clubs and organizations.

Put systems in place to consistently solicit employee suggestions for improving the organization. After all, they are the people on the front lines actually doing the work, building the parts, and servicing the customers. Put out employee suggestion boxes, and ask for suggestions during staff meetings. Once the ideas are gathered, there must also be a systematic way of analyzing ideas to see which should be tested and implemented.

Analyzing Improvement Ideas

Obviously every suggestion will not be usable, at least not immediately. So a process must be developed for analyzing which ideas should be pursued. Again, involving employees in the process is vital, especially if management wants the employees to accept ownership of the changes which will result from the new ideas.

One organization we work with has a quality steering committee. This committee includes one or two individuals from each department in the company. Part of the committee's responsibility is to analyze suggestions made by employees, and make recommendations for implementation.

Implementing Improvement Ideas

For the process to work, some of the ideas must be implemented. Organizations can't just talk the talk; they must also walk the walk. If employee suggestions are never implemented, employees will eventually assume that their input is not truly valued.

Employee suggestions should be included in the organization's planning process. When setting goals and developing strategies, leadership should be asking, "How can we implement the ideas that have come from the people on the front line."

REWARD EXCELLENCE IN THE WORKPLACE

Organization's desiring to improve employee satisfaction need a system in place which consistently rewards employee achievements.

I'm always surprised how few organizations have such a system. Three key approaches to rewarding excellence and improving employee satisfaction include: appreciation, recognition, and compensation.

Appreciation

Many times, positive behaviors and achievements are not acknowledged by leadership, so people don't know whether or not they are doing a good job. I recently had an employee of an organization tell me, "The only time we ever hear anything from management is when we do something wrong." Employers can improve employee satisfaction levels by rewarding employees with personal attention; a pat on the back, a hand-written note, or a quick comment in the hall.

When showing appreciation, be specific. Instead of just saying, "We really are grateful for the good job you do around here," the approach might be, "I really appreciate how you handled the Franklin Industries account last week when we had to get their rush order out late Friday afternoon. Your effort really made a difference." By being specific, the employer comes across as much more sincere, and the employee realizes their actions are truly being watched.

Recognition

Many people will do for recognition what they will not do for money. Strange, but true. Some people are motivated by the opportunity to get their name on the wall, receive a trophy at an annual banquet, or see their name in the company newsletter. It gives them an "emotional payoff" for their actions.

Look for ways to recognize excellence in the workplace. Ring a bell every time an individual or team hits the production target. Put up posters with the photographs of team members who have had the most days without accidents. Give out awards for attendance records. Just do something. It is so inexpensive, yet highly effective.

Compensation

Some people are motivated by money. In fact, most people, are motivated by money; at least for their basic needs. Compensation can come in the form of raises, performance bonuses, commissions, profit sharing, or any number of "extra benefits" like, automobiles, vacations, or other tangible items purchased and used as rewards.

I noticed an interesting program in a hotel where I recently stayed. They have a sophisticated system for rewarding employees based on customer feedback. Throughout the hotel, they have placed customer feedback forms and boxes for depositing the forms. When customers comment on the performance of a hotel employee, the employee accumulates points which can be used to purchase rewards like trips, gifts, and other incentives.

Whatever the chosen method, it is important to have a system in place which rewards people's efforts with some type of additional compensation. Not every person is motivated by the same factor, or combination of factors. Offering appreciation, recognition, AND compensation insures that the organization has something to contribute to the satisfaction of each employee.

MONITOR EMPLOYEE SATISFACTION

Two levels of satisfaction should be monitored regularly. The first is customer satisfaction, and the second is employee satisfaction. Many organizations are committed to the former, but few have any system in place to monitor the latter. They should. Because, if the levels of customer satisfaction, performance, or productivity are low, there's a pretty good chance employee satisfaction levels are low.

Don't Wait

Don't wait for exit interviews to identify why people are dissatisfied in the organization. It's too late then. And, don't depend on "the grapevine" either. Develop a system for monitoring employee satisfaction levels. The system can be as informal as pulling everyone together on a monthly or quarterly basis to solicit ideas on how to help them be more successful and fulfilled in their jobs. Employers might speak one-on-one with employees, or have each manager speak to the people in their department. Monitoring employee satisfaction levels provides a powerful tool for identifying weaknesses in the organization, and helps determine if the organization is a morale builder or a morale buster.

CHAPTER SEVEN

If You Can't Say Anything Nice... What Do You Say?

How to give constructive criticism or confront negative situations without destroying employee performance.

Sarita Maybin

Sarita Maybin is an award-winning professional speaker who has trained thousands of people in 46 of the 50 states, in nine Canadian provinces, in England, Hong Kong, Singapore and Malaysia.

Sarita's expertise and previous experience includes a Masters Degree in Counseling and thirteen years as a supervisor in Higher Education.

Sarita offers customized training solutions...or you can select from one of her four most popular programs.

Seminars & Keynote Speeches for your Communication Challenges:

- How to Turn Negativity into Possibility... At Work and Beyond
- Total Teamwork
- How to Get More Done with Less Stress
- Communicating for Success

Sarita Maybin
Oceanside, CA • (760) 758-3155 • www.SaritaTalk.com

Sarita Maybin

If You Can't Say Anything Nice...
What Do You Say?

How to give constructive criticism or confront negative situations without destroying employee performance.

We've always been told if we can't say anything nice, we should not say anything at all. Yet, there are times, especially at work, when we may need to give constructive criticism or confront a negative situation. If our goal is improved employee performance and productivity, it benefits us to know how to constructively give negative feedback.

In this chapter we will discuss:
- Why it is so difficult for us to confront employees (and colleagues too, for that matter)...and how to get over it
- Do's and Don'ts of Giving Constructive Criticism
- Ten phrases that promote positive communication
- Three step process for giving negative feedback
- How to quantify bad attitude in order to hold an employee accountable

First, why is it so difficult for us to confront negative behavior? There seems to be an unlimited supply of reasons not to confront. What if they become defensive? What if I'm making a big deal out of nothing? What if I hurt their feelings? What if I make matters worse?

According to the authors of Difficult Conversations, the recently published book based on the work of the Harvard Negotiation Project, "No matter how good you get, difficult conversations will always challenge you. Achieving perfect results without risk will not happen. Getting better results in the face of tolerable odds might." In other words, there will always be risk in confrontation, but with the use of certain strategies and skills, we have a better change of getting the results we want.

As supervisors, confronting negative behavior is part of the job. One way to motivate ourselves to confront difficult situations is to ask the question Why do I want to confront this person? Just because "their way" isn't "my way" is not necessarily a good reason to confront. However, if "their" way is negatively affecting us or the performance of those around us, we may want to confront the situation. In fact, there are times when we may need to confront, especially if there are safety or health issues involved.

When I recently asked participants in one of my seminars "What's in it for us to confront a negative situation"?" Some of their answers include:

- make employee aware of the problem
- there may actually be improvement
- keep the problem from getting worse
- reduce resentment from other employees
- keeps the behavior from becoming a norm

These are all good reasons for us to acknowledge our fear of confronting...and get over it! And, if these are not reason enough to confront, it may be helpful to know the results of an national employee survey which asked "What most bothers you about where you work?" The answer: "People are getting away with things and no one is doing anything about it". This suggests that other employees resent it when supervisors don't confront unproductive and disruptive behaviors in the workplace.

So, how do we confront employees in a constructive way? Following are "Do's and "Don'ts" that may be helpful:

Do's and Don'ts of Constructive Confrontation

DO:

- Treat the person with dignity (even if their behavior has consistently annoyed us)
- Discuss in private
- Use "I" statements ("I'm concerned", "I need you to", "I would appreciate")
- Seek clarification ("Help me understand your concerns regarding the project")
- Confirm understanding ("So what you're saying is...")
- Explain how the behavior affects others ("When you come late, others have to wait")
- Seek solutions ("How can we resolve this", "Would you be willing to")
- Maintain perspective/sense of humor

DON'T:

- Don't point finger or blame
- Don't make it personal
- If possible, don't confront in front of others
- Don't dictate or use "you" statements (avoid "You should", "You better", "You need to")
- Don't drop hints or use sarcasm
- Don't argue
- Don't name names (if they say "who told you that", say "that's not important" and re-focus)
- Don't expect immediate change

To set a positive tone when giving negative feedback, try out the top ten positive communication phrases below. These ten phrases also demonstrate four important guidelines for giving negative feedback which you may have also noticed in the Do's and Don'ts just reviewed.

Top 10 Positive Communication Phrases

Guideline 1: Give other person benefit of the doubt

10. "You may not realize..."
9. "Are you aware of how this affects..."

Guideline 2: Seek input

8. "Help me understand..."
7. "I need your help..."
6. "I noticed...and I'm wondering..."
5. "Would you be willing to..."

Guideline 3: Take responsibility

4. "I'm concerned..."
3. "I would appreciate..."

Guideline 4: Work together

2. "How can we resolve this..."
1. "What will it take..."

I've got two favorites on this list of phrases. You may also find favorites on this list that you think will actually work for you.

#8 - "Help me understand...." is my first favorite phrase. You may recognize that phrase from the bumbling, but brilliant TV detective Colombo. Remember how he would say "I'm confused, help me understand...I thought we agreed..." His non-threatening posture made it easy for people NOT to feel defensive around him. And, he was more likely to get the information and results he wanted. Personally, I feel like I've spent much of my professional life being Colombo. For example:

"Help me understand your concerns about the project"
"Help me understand what happened; I thought we agreed
    the project would be done by Friday"
"Help me understand how you feel this should be handled"

One of the nice things about this phrase is that it is exactly the opposite of the unproductive, blaming phrases that we are tempted to use. For example, "Help me understand" gets better results than "I'm gonna make YOU understand".

Another one of my favorites on this list is #6 "I noticed...and I'm wondering..." This is a great neutral multi-purpose phrase which allows us to point out our observations and then seek additional information or input from the other person....without pointing the finger or blaming. Consider these examples:

> "I noticed that you were late and I'm wondering
>   what happened"
> "I noticed that the project was not completed and
>   I'm wondering what went wrong"
> "I noticed that you sighed when we mentioned the project
>   and I'm wondering how I should interpret that"
> "I noticed that you've mentioned several problems and
>   I'm wondering what solutions you've considered"

I recall the unfortunate incident shared by one of my seminar participants who had recently received a performance appraisal from her supervisor. She told me that he said to her "you're not a team player". When she asked for specific examples he said "you sit in staff meetings with closed body posture". In other words, she sat at meetings with her arms folded. What might be another reason for that? Exactly! She was cold! How often do we make assumptions with our employees and with each other? That's why seeking input by saying, for example, "I noticed that you're arms are folded and I'm wondering how I should interpret that?" may keep us from looking foolish when we make incorrect assumptions.

A Model For Feedback

Let's look at yet another approach for giving negative feedback. This is a three step model:
1. Awareness
2. Affect
3. Action

The most valuable application of this three step model is in confronting "bad attitudes". As you probably know, we can't hold anyone accountable for a bad attitude. We must point out the specific behavior, or quantify, the attitude. Plus, it's even more useful if we can explain how that behavior affects others (step 2 above).

Let's look at a typical scenario:

Pat is a hard worker and generally turns in quality and timely assignments. She has even been acknowledged as Employee of the Month on two occasions. In fact, senior management views her favorably and has even praised her at management meetings.

However, Pat has a habit of complaining to you and others about how awful things are and how no one really appreciates her hard work. She says it's only a matter of time before she finds a better job and leaves, even though she has been employed there for 15 years. Further, she spreads rumors, gossips and naysays. "That will never work", "Why Change it now?"and"That's a stupid idea" are frequent phrases in her conversation.

So, how do we confront her? What phrases might result in the most positive outcome? As you can tell, there are a few issues to be addressed here. First, the fact that she never feels appreciated. Second, that her naysaying is probably negatively affecting others. Third, her gossiping and spreading rumors is creating misinformation and stress among the staff. This is where the three step model comes in handy. Let's look at possible options:

Issue I - Pat not feeling appreciated/complaining

STEP ONE- Awareness

"Pat, do you realize that you mention feeling unappreciated frequently, yet you have received two employee of the month awards and we feel you are an important part of our team"

STEP TWO- Affect

"Your co-workers find it frustrating that you continue to be acknowledged, yet don't seem to ever feel that anything around here is good enough."

STEP THREE - Action

"What will it take to have you understand that we really DO appreciate your efforts?"

ISSUE II- Pat's naysaying

STEP ONE - Awareness

"I'm wondering if you are aware of the fact that you frequently say things like 'that won't work" or 'that's a stupid' idea"

STEP TWO -

"I'm concerned that others feel put down or discounted when you say that"

STEP THREE-

"I would appreciate your not making these types of comments in the future. Or, at least explain your concerns rather than abruptly dismissing others' ideas."

ISSUE III- Pat's spreading rumors, gossiping

STEP ONE- Awareness

"It's come to my attention that there is information about other employees and the company that is being shared that is not completely accurate. Your name keeps coming up in relation to this.

STEP TWO - Affect

"...I'm concerned that this misinformation is causing others to feel anxious and uncertain about the company's future and that employees are becoming distracted by this."

STEP THREE - Action

"If you are involved, I'd like to hear your thoughts on how we can stop the spread of this misinformation. If you're NOT involved and there is just a perception that you are, then, how might we get rid of that perception?

I'm sure that by now the little voice in the back of your head is saying "Well, this sounds good. But what if the employee is not buying into what I'm saying?" Obviously, there are no guarantees that the employee will respond favorably. We stated that at the beginning of this chapter. However, you may have noticed some common themes in the phrasing that will increase our chances of getting a favorable response:

- Non-blaming "I" statements rather than the blaming "You" statements
- When possible, we sought the employees perspective and input

- We gave them the benefit of the doubt
- When possible, we acknowledged our appreciation of the employee

As you can probably guess, a lot of the employee's reaction will be a result of how we have previously interacted with them and the type of environment we have created. Following is a "reality check" to see whether we have set the stage for positive interaction. If you answer "no" to any of these items, that might suggest an area where an employee may have a legitimate concern.

___1. Employees feel free to express concerns directly to their supervisor

___2. Employees receive on going positive and negative feedback

___3. Structured opportunities to provide suggestions are used by employees

___4. Employees are able to work out concerns and conflicts with each other

___5. Employees generally feel positive about their workplace

___6. Training on how to communicate and resolve conflict has been provided for employees

___7. There has been relatively LOW employee turnover during the last several years (high turnover or change would cause employees to feel stressed, anxious and respond less favorably)

___8. Employees generally care about the quality of their work

___9. New ideas and suggestions are generally accepted and if possible, acted upon

___10.Rewards and recognition are provided for hard work

Once we've set a positive state, we have many specific tools to use that help us encourage improved employee performance and productivity. The top ten phrases, do's and don'ts of giving constructive criticism and a three-step model for giving negative feedback are a good start.

Now, if you can't say anything nice, you DO know what to say...and do!

CHAPTER EIGHT

CA$H in on Generation X

How to get the best from young talent.

Rebecca S. Morgan

CBS, Citibank, and financial service providers call Rebecca Morgan "exciting," "awesome," and "energetic." Rebecca's fresh, feisty perspective on managing and marketing to young people has earned her the title, "The Harvard Business Review...on Rollerblades." Rebecca's delivery knocks starch from stuffed shirts and keeps audiences buzzing.

Rebecca's firm, neXt generation consulting, was born on April Fools Day, 1998 - no fooling. neXt generation consulting helps organizations "tune-up" their management and marketing strategies. Rebecca is author of a forthcoming book, *Xtreme Leadership, a profile of America's Gen X leaders.*

Rebecca earned degrees in Economics and International Relations from Drake University, and played professional basketball in Europe. She has been featured on the cover of the Des Moines Business Record, and her articles have appeared in Financial Services Journal.

Best selling keynotes include:
- Leadership Lessons from the Professional Basketball Bench
- Marketing to the MTV Generation
- Slackers to Superstars: Managing Young Employees

Rebecca S. Morgan
Minneapolis, MN • (888) 922-9596 • www.rebeccaspeaks.com

Rebecca S. Morgan

CA$H in on Generation X

How to get the best from young talent.

Did you get the Memo? You know, the one with the subject, "Employee Loyalty is Dead"? It was dated in the mid-1980's. The Memo is one of the reasons that Gen Xers are changing jobs every 18 months.

Lots of organizations say they never got the Memo. That's why they're pouring obscene amounts of money into recruiting, bonuses, and retention. Here's a reprint. Please circulate it in your office.

MEMO

Date: 1984 [circa the AT&T announcement to eliminate 21,000 jobs, spurring the largest corporate restructuring in history]

To: Organizations that rely on talent

Subj: Employee Loyalty is Dead

Loyalty among employees will die. Corporations will kill it. In this decade GM, IBM, AT&T, US West and others will cut 3.4 million jobs in the U.S.

It will be called "down-sizing," "right-sizing" or "re-engineering." Whatever you call it, the massive lay-offs of the 1980's and subsequent recession will cut a deep gash in America's security blanket. The millions of people who loose their jobs will not just be "unnecessary overhead costs." They will be parents of a new generation of employees, Generation X.

After the lay-offs, to make ends meet, parents will head back to work – BOTH of them. Without after-school supervision, America's first generation of Latchkey kids will come of age. They will learn to rely on themselves to set the table, set the VCR, and set the agenda for "quality time" with their parents.

Despite the evidence that employee loyalty will die, some organizations won't let go. They will keep Loyalty on life support, pumping more dollars, benefits, and retention plans into the feeding tubes. They believe that if they pray long enough at its bedside, Employee Loyalty will begin breathing on its own again. Don't get caught in this trap. Employee Loyalty will die. Move on.

There you have it in black and white: the Memo. Now that you've read it for yourself, maybe it will be easier to see Generation X for what they are – the first generation of New Economy employees to come of age relying on themselves – not corporations – for employment security.

Seth Godin describes it as Free Agent Nation. Gen Xers are a huge pool of temporary employees. They don't leave their jobs. They find new opportunities. There's a difference. Gen Xers rely on themselves to build a portfolio of skills, networks, and project credentials that will serve them in any job.

So, instead of praying at the bedside of Employee Loyalty, turn your thoughts to the New Economy employment issues you can affect.

In this chapter, I will explain:
- Why the genetic code of young employees seems so different from veteran talent
- How to cut the learning curve so new employees are profitable faster

How is Gen X Different? The Four S's

Today's young people are lazy, disloyal, slackers. That's what the media says. Over 75 percent of media coverage about Generation X is negative.

Some of you probably agree with the media's portrayal of Gen X. I don't blame you. Here's a short list of the things clients tell me drive them NUTS about Generation X [b. 1961-1980.]

- It took Gen Xers five years to get a four year degree
- Gen Xers pierce and tattoo their bodies in places we wish they wouldn't
- Gen Xers are missing the part of the genetic code that stimulates ironing or tucking in their clothes
- When they finally show up at work, Gen Xers frequently ask, "Why do we do it this way?"
- "CD" means compact disc – not certificate of deposit - to Gen Xers
- Gen Xers expect senior management positions within five minutes of college graduation

But organizations aren't totally sour on this generation either. Gen Xers are flexible, they love training, they're risk-takers, they learn 4-5 new software titles each year, and they can program a VCR with one hand tied behind their back. Gen Xers are the first Americans who grew up with Apples™ that have memories!

For better or worse, Gen Xers are here to stay. Gen Xers are not going to be replaced by people who act more like your parents. Right behind Generation X is Generation Y (also known as "Nexters," "Echo Boomers," or "Millennials"). Gen Y is even more technically savvy, demanding, and creative!

Leaders must learn what makes the New Economy employee tick. Why? Because Gen X turnover is a slow, steady blood-letting of human capital. It cripples productivity and growth. Finding replacements swells recruiting budgets. Turnover can be prevented, but you have to be willing to learn tricks from the New Economy employment playbook.

So let's look at what makes young talent tick. Following are four S's of Generation X. These are the cornerstones of understanding the world Gen Xers grew up in, and why they act the way they do.

Skeptical Gen Xers

Skeptical Gen Xers came of age as American institutions were crumbling. The Iran-Contra scandal, declining U.S. scores in math and science, the Challenger explosion, corporate downsizing and unemployment, high divorce rates, razorblades in Halloween candy, and faces of missing children were headlines as Gen X children came of age in the 1960's, 70's and 80's. The result? A generation of young people who don't talk to strangers and rely on themselves. Gen Xers are skeptical. You have to earn their trust and respect.

Savvy Gen Xers

Savvy Gen Xers were raised on a steady diet of technology and information. Video games, computers, and cable television exposed them to millions of megabytes of electronic stimuli, available 24 hours a day. This generation has no recall of the "old days" when all three networks went gray at 11 PM to the sounds of the National Anthem. Today's young employees choose from hundreds of television channels, have access to millions of books, and online resources beyond number. They have adapted to the information overload, and learned to manage it. This is the bullet-point generation. They don't read long memos; they prefer short, get-to-the-point emails. Gen Xers use technology and other resources to sift through gobs of information and make informed decisions. They're info- and tech-savvy.

Self-reliant Gen Xers

The Self-reliant 40 percent of Gen Xers were raised in single parent households. This is America's first generation of latchkey children. They learned how to set the VCR, set the table, and set the agenda for what they wanted from dad on weekend visits. This generation is highly self-sufficient and can take care of themselves. Don't micromanage them. They want responsibility and credit for doing a good job. Generation X is our first consumer group of multi-taskers. From early ages, they were watching TV, doing their homework, talking on the phone with friends, and having a snack. They rely on themselves to build the skills and networks that will take them from the break room to the boardroom.

Swift Gen Xers

Swift Gen Xers like fast computers, quick turn-around time and instant access. Gen Xers don't wait for organizations to open. They do research, apply for loans, and comparison shop electronically, preferring to search online than wait inline. Gen Xers do face to face banking less than twice per year. Why? It's not convenient. And convenience is the name of the game. Gen Xers want to streamline their lives, to make things simpler, and swifter.

Cut the Learning Curve

I think it was SHRM (Society for Human Resource Management) where I first read that it takes employees six months to get up and running in their new jobs. Art Dinkin at 4Sight Financial Services, a Gen X financial planning firm, says it takes most agents two years before they're contributing anything to the bottom line.

Twenty years ago – in the old economy - spending six to twenty-four months getting an employee up to speed was a good investment because they stayed for a looooong time. My dad worked 33 years in a row at the West Bend Company before he took early retirement (read: "down-sizing") in the late 1980's. Thirty-three years is a darn good return on a six-month investment.

But it's a crappy investment in today's New Economy employment market.

In the Old Economy, we asked, "How can we make employees stay longer?" The New Economy question is, "How can we make young employees profitable faster?"

The First Day

In today's hyper-speed, A.D.D. economy, young talent sizes you up quickly. Making a great first impression is the first step to cutting the learning curve.

Gen Xers I interview say that the First Day usually includes:
- Filling out employment forms in the HR office
- Reading the P&P (Policy and Procedure) Handbook

- A company tour with a friendly, overworked administrative assistant
- Sitting through a short "welcome aboard" meeting with their manager

That's it. Often, Gen Xers start new jobs in temporary quarters. They don't get telephones, access to the building, and login pass codes for the computer system, or meetings with supervisor and work teams for weeks. If this happens in your organization, you're making a very bad first impression on young talent.

If you want your young talent to hit the ground running in their new jobs, you need to provide them with the tools and resources to do their job on the first day.

One west coast technology firm has this riddle figured out. When a manager hires a new employee, they fill out an online form with the new employee's bio, start date, position, salary and bonus structure, technology required, work space requirement, pass code requests, and a mentor request.

This form is e-mailed to the Chief Operating Officer (COO) who sets in motion all the events that must be coordinated to assemble the work space, get the right technology ordered and networked, process the passwords, recruit a mentor, and post the new employee bio online so everyone can welcome them aboard when they start.

One week before the new employee starts, they receive a bouquet of flowers, a welcome note from the President and senior staff, and a packet of HR forms that they are asked to fill out and bring on their first day.

On their first day, the new employee has breakfast on-site with their mentor. The mentor tells their story about their employment at the company and talks about future opportunities for growth. They agree on goals for the mentoring relationship.

The mentor takes them on a tour – including the HR department where the forms are dropped off – introduces them to their workspace where they set up email and voicemail accounts, and goes through the corporate library where on-site training takes place. The new employee receives a workbook with questions about the company, the products and services they provide, as well as policies and procedures. This workbook must be completed within 2 weeks.

The new employee lunches with their manager, who shares the

new employee's job description, first project assignments, and asks for feedback. They talk about how success is measured, and agree on an appointment for the 2-week employee review. The manager explains her "open door" management principle: when you need help, ask. From that point on, the employee joins step with their project team.

Time after time, Gen Xers refer to their first day orientation as one of the things that attracted them to this firm. The first day orientation helps Gen Xers hit the ground running with the tools (technology, job description, project assignment, policies and procedures, and a mentor) to get productive fast.

New Employee Orientation Checklist

Here's a checklist of items to include in New Employee Orientation:

- A real life, real time message from the President including a Q&A session. [Starbucks uses a video of their president welcoming them and outlining what Starbucks stands for. On-site managers handle Q&A.]
- Story Time: why we're here, who we serve, how your work has meaning
- Personalized passwords to access email, intranet, web, and voicemail
- Schedule for their first evaluation and a fresh, accurate job description that outlines how they'll be evaluated
- Introduction to their mentor
- Overview of all the training programs available to employees, and how to sign up

1. *Rekindling Commitment: How to revitalize yourself, your work, and your organization,* by Dennis T. Jaffe, Cynthia D. Scott, and Glenn R. Tobe, © 1994, Jossey-Bass, San Francisco, CA, p. 14

2. Based on the books *Managing Generation X* and *The Manager's Pocket Guide to Generation X* by Bruce Tulgan

CHAPTER NINE

The Hidden Performance Factor

How to boost employee performance by discovering each individual's underlying drive.

Bette Price, CPBA

Bette Price is a recognized expert in the field of value-based performance. As a consultant she challenges the status quo to ignite new ways of thinking. As a professional speaker she brings real life experience to the platform when she speaks on the topics of performance alignment, marketing, leadership, and change.

She is president of The Price Group, a consulting firm that helps companies maximize success by improving performance and managing the intangible impact of change.

Price is certified in the science of measuring why and how companies perform. She works with companies to analyze and define the core values that drive the company, and designs marketing, management and hiring strategies which ensure that planning decisions are aligned with core values to maximize performance and growth.

Price brings more than twenty years of experience to her clients. Since 1982, she has worked with small to mid-sized engineering, telecommunications, health care and environmental businesses as well as such major corporations as IBM Global Services, Alcatel, and Sony Electronics.

The Price Group
Addison, TX • (972) 404-0787 • www.pricegroupmarketing.com

Bette Price, CPBA

The Hidden Performance Factor

How to boost employee performance by discovering each individual's underlying drive.

Have you even been disappointed by an employee who seemed just right for the position, yet failed to perform to your expectations? Is your company making a profit, yet you know the potential is even greater? Would you like to eliminate some of the day-to-day management issues that eat up your time? Could your bottom line be improved if you didn't have to worry about employee turn-over? And, could the overall environment of your workplace be boosted a bit?

If you answered "yes" to two or more of these questions, chances are you have a performance problem. And, even though your company may be profitable, you have likely not begun to maximize success. Achieving maximum success is all about performance. Performance is all about motivation, and motivation is driven by basic core values. Every company's driving force stems from its leaders' values. It is what we have come to know as the company culture. Take General Electric for example. There's little question that CEO Jack Welch greatly values results, profits, quality and having his company seen as an industry leader. He expects leading edge performance from his management team and he likes the limelight. Jack Welch is GE. Not so with Maytag, Whirlpool, and any number of other competitors. You don't see their CEOs writing books and developing leadership training programs that are gobbled up by other corporations who are striving to duplicate some small part of the success Welsh has created for GE.

You may be saying to yourself, 'now hold on, Price. You're not implying that these other CEOs don't want profits too,' are you? Of course they want profits. But they are probably less passionate about profitable results, image, and quality than Jack Welch. It's the intensity and combination that establishes a culture that accepts nothing less than the best. Employees of GE who embrace similar values will feel like they work in a culture that fits their interests, attitudes and values. They will be the achievers and they will likely be the ones who reap the rewards of upward mobility within the corporate structure. Employees who embrace other values may do well in certain aspects of their careers, but may tend to feel conflict in other areas. At some point of dissatisfaction, these are the individuals who will leave the company. Most often they will say it's for a better opportunity to make more money. Rarely is that the real, underlying reason.

Aptitude, experience, and education are all important factors that help to predict how the individual will perform a specific job. However, why an individual is motivated to put aptitude, experience, and education to work with all their gusto, is often overlooked. Therein lies the problem. We have not discovered the individual's underlying drive -- the Hidden Performance Factor. Think of it this way. A child may be born with an inherent gift for music and with early training may learn to play the piano with great skill. However, if the child has little interest (value) in playing piano, potential success will not be maximized. When we explore Maslow's Hierarchy of Needs, it is understandable why people often fall into a trap of taking a job because it pays well. While money is to some degree a motivator, it is rarely the major motivator. Thus, when the money is good, but the fit is not, performance suffers.

A Wrong Hire for the Culture and Need

Norman (not his real name) is an example of this trap. Norman is well educated. He has an engineering degree and he has been gifted with strong people skills, an asset in a part-time counseling job. Following a divorce, Norman combined multiple projects to generate enough income to meet his new financial commitments. Then one day he encountered a job possibility that would provide more security – marketing director for a small environmental engineering firm. Norman did great during the interview. His engineering degree was an asset, he had previous industry experience, and he was extremely personable. He even convinced the company's officers that he could be a great salesman. After all, he had sold himself on all the entrepreneurial projects he had been handling. Selling was important because the main thing the company needed from this marketing manager was to quickly generate sales. No doubt about it, Norman told them convincingly. So they hired him.

Weeks passed. Norman developed new information sheets to take to prospects, he developed tracking systems on the computer, and he created an elaborate sales call form to evaluate each sales call he would make. Would make. That's right; for weeks Norman was so busy getting ready that he never actually made a sales call. Finally the president called for action. Norman reluctantly got on the phone, made appointments and called on some prospects. When he returned to the office he spent considerable time writing long, detailed reports of the calls he had made. Then he ranked each prospect, using his own ranking system of one to ten, with ten denoting strong possibility of a sale. From the sales calls made by Norman, he ranked none higher than three. Not too promising for a small company that needed quick results.

Only after considerable time and money was spent on this non-productive employee did the company leadership discover that they and Norman did not have shared and aligned values. What Norman valued was taking time to get to know customers, being very service-oriented, gathering lots of information and detailing that information for future use. All admirable characteristics, but not well matched for a company that valued-- and needed—action, return on investment and quick results. The hiring mistake was emotionally and financially costly for both Norman and the company. After several agonizing months and numerous attempts to give Norman encouragement and help, performance not only failed to improve – it never came. Finally, Norman was fired.

What could the company have done to see that Norman was not a right fit? How could Norman himself have spotted the misfit? Each now know. They could have looked beneath the visible factors like experience, education and skill. By using a value-based assessment they could easily have determined if Norman had interests, attitudes, and values that were aligned with those of the company's key leadership. Even without an assessment to provide tangible insight, more highly focused interviewing and listening during the interview process would have revealed indications that Norman would not likely be able to perform the quick results that were expected and needed. Reality came to light for this company after-the-fact when the leadership decided to assess the entire leadership and management team. Quick results, turning on a dime, ensuring quality in a timely manner, and practical performance were high on the value list for the core leadership team. Quick turn-around was even a promise made to customers. For the sales and marketing position quick results was more than expected, it was demanded. For Norman, none of these motivators were a fit. Norman would have been a valuable employee in a role that allowed him time to build relationships that would eventually result in sales. Had the company employed a large, sales force that was already generating strong income, perhaps Norman could have been given time to cultivate relationships with prospects. With extended time, Norman may well have generated sales and attracted very loyal customers. But, because the company was small, they didn't have the luxury of allowing Norman's long nurturing approach. Even if the company could have financially withstood the long-term development, the strong values mismatch would have kept Norman from feeling like a valued part of the management team. . His slow-growth attitude would have been in constant conflict with leadership's attitude of quick-growth.

This example merely mirrors thousands of situations that exist in diverse industries and in both large and small organizations. At one major commercial mortgage company, the division president and the key leadership team spent hours developing a mission from which the division would operate. When our organization was called upon during the second month of operation to assist with some additional planning, we assessed the entire leadership team. When comparing the results it became clear that the entire mission they had developed was incongruent with the actual values and expectations that motivated the leadership team. The president quickly realized that while the words read well, they were meaningless to future planning for growth and direction. The words failed to reflect the core values, thus they had written an empty mission statement. We were asked to facilitate a rework of the mission statement so that words would be aligned with core values and that future goals and objectives would be realistically aligned with the same core values. Upon completion it was remarkably enlightening to the entire team that if they had planned from the previously crafted mission statement, the plan would have taken them totally off track from who they truly were and what they really wanted to accomplish.

In another corporation, a new manager asked for help to ensure that engineers were placed on the appropriate teams to reduce frustration and dissatisfaction, and, ultimately, to reduce turnover. With core competencies identified, we used assessment results to make recommendations. Some engineers were motivated by the challenge of using their knowledge to create new systems and resolves while others were more traditional and systematic in the application of their knowledge. This hidden information was extremely useful in helping to place engineers with seemingly similar qualifications on the teams that enabled them to best use their knowledge and feel personal fulfillment. As a result, this manager has reduced dissatisfaction, improved morale, and reduced turnover. Performance has been maximized.

Research Support

According to a Michigan State University study, ninety percent of all hiring decisions are culminated through the interview, yet interviews only produce 14 percent accuracy. Assessments that probe beneath experience, education and skills provide this missing piece. The average assessment can cost as little as $75-- a small price to pay for avoiding a wrong-fit decision. One major bank calculated that replacing a $17,000 employee because a poor hiring decision was made would cost the company $51,000. Experts say the same hiring mistake with a manager costs the company three times the manager's annual salary. You do the numbers. With one $75,000 manager mistake, we're talking real money. When these types of hiring mistakes are made within large corporations, poor performance costs often get hidden among other cost factors. The danger here is that inappropriate changes are often made to try to fix the problem, further delaying the expected performance. Mid to small sized businesses don't have this luxury. When small companies make these types of mistakes, poor performance will quickly show up as a major bleed to the bottom line.

Successful Performance Is Predictable

Despite the onset of modern technology, today's performance success remains highly dependent upon people. First, the people who lead the business; next the people hired to accomplish the tasks of the business. Here are some steps to consider to help maximize your company's performance:

1. Consider using a scientific assessment tool to validate the hidden attitudes and motivators that are key to you and your leadership team. Our company uses a patented product that clearly identifies six key business values/motivators. Costs are minimal for the insight provided.

2. If you don't use an assessment, do some strong soul searching with an objective colleague to identify "why" you are in business beyond the money factor. Or, in the case of a corporate division head, why you show up for work each day.

From the following six categories, which two or three are most passionately important to you?

Knowledge.

A strong desire for constant learning. To be seen as knowledgeable and to be recognized for your knowledge and expertise. A strong desire to use your knowledge in a growth-oriented and meaningful way.

Results and Practicality.

A practical mind-set that demands return on investment and expects timely results. Action-oriented and result-oriented. Your motto could well be, "get it done, get it done right, and get it done now."

People First.

A strong belief that people must come first, sometimes to your own detriment. Service, assistance, and helping others is at the forefront of all you do.

Emotionally Energized.

An intangible feeling or instinct that drives decisions. Emotionally tied to decisions. Decisions frequently made on "gut feelings," because it feels right. Intense emotional love of the industry, product, or service involved. Creative outlets to express highly felt emotions.

Quality and Image.

A strong desire to be viewed as a leader in your field. To be seen only in the best light. To demand quality and to expect visible evidence of quality in all aspects of the business. To be seen first for quality performance.

Established.

Strongly held beliefs that remain ever-present regardless of changing times. Traditional thinking. Cautious when introducing new concepts or ideas. Firm about maintaining elements of the old while transitioning into something new.

Application

Select no more than three categories that best fit your beliefs. Elements of these mind-sets will be the strongest motivators that drive your company or division. If similar beliefs are not held by those who work for and with you, expect performance conflicts. As a leader, it is vitally important to reflect these core elements in your mission statement and in everything you do to convey your expectations for performance. When interviewing, it is important to ask open-ended questions that will demand responses that reveal the individual's fit with your core value expectations. Do more listening than talking. It is amazing how much will be revealed in the interview process if you truly listen for key motivators and attitudes. All the skills and intellect in the world will not compensate for the wrong attitude.

Finally, be sure that the words and images used to attract customers are reflective of your core values. This is a marketing issue that will directly impact the success of your marketing performance. When your marketing messages attract customers who are not aligned with your key values you will find it more difficult to complete the sale and more difficult to retain and please them long-term. Just like employees, when the core values are more ideally aligned, relationships flourish and you are more likely to have satisfied customers for life.

The hidden value factors – whether they are issues of hiring, managing, or marketing, will ultimately determine how well you will maximize performance with both your people and your bottom line. Remember, achieving maximum success is all about performance. Performance is all about motivation, and motivation is driven by basic core values – specifically yours, when you are in charge.

CHAPTER TEN

You Can Become An Energizer!

Strategies for creating an energized workforce.

Gary Rifkin

Gary Rifkin, also known as "THE ENERGIZER", has been working in the training and speaking business for over 15 years. His enthusiastic style has helped him build the confidence and competence of folks in a variety of settings. His keynote speeches have been described as both inspiring and fun. Gary's new audio tape series, "Grandma Says..." is getting rave reviews. The first tape in the series, "Feel Good, Do Good, Be Good" is the basis for his upcoming book "The Mensch".

In addition to dynamic keynotes, Gary also leads seminars in Presentation Skills, Team Building, Innovation & Creativity, Meyers-Briggs, and a variety of other performance improvement areas. He serves as a Senior Associate with The Pennington Performance Group and teaches Time Power for Cannonwood, DayTimer's Training Partner.

Gary has worked with organizations including UPS, Ericsson, Johnson & Johnson, Fujitsu, World Travel Partners, The City of Irving and Baylor University. He has a Bachelors degree from Penn State University and a Masters from Bowling Green State University. Gary is an active member of the National Speakers Association and was chosen Member of the Year by its North Texas Chapter.

Rifkin Training & Consulting
Dallas, TX • 1-877-FYI-GARY • www.RifkinTraining.com

<u>Gary Rifkin</u>

You Can Become An Energizer

Strategies for creating an energized workforce.

Main Entry: **en·er·gize**
Function: *verb*
  - to make energetic, vigorous, or active; to impart energy to

One of the most important factors in improving employee productivity and performance is insuring an energized workforce. Interestingly enough, it's also one of the easiest things to do! Let's look at a few strategies for energizing folks.

Showing Respect

By far the most necessary trait in becoming an "energizer" is showing respect.

I do training on sexual harassment. Instead of it being the usual, boring list of things you're not allowed to do, I've designed the entire program around the concept of professionalism.

One of the first activities in the class is to have small groups of students brainstorm the qualities and characteristics of a professional. Without fail, one of the most critical characteristics listed is respect. In fact, the majority of the qualities usually relate to respect in some way. It's no secret that employees who feel respected by their employer have greater loyalty and are better motivated to be successful.

So how do you show respect?

Well, you can always fall back on the tried and true golden rule. Treat others the way you'd want to be treated. Will this work? Not necessarily!

You see, the golden rule, in principle, means to treat everyone with respect. But let's take it literally. Is it okay for me to treat people the way I want to be treated? I'm a hugger. When I first greet people, I like to hug them. What if I came up to you, having never met you before and gave you a big bear hug. Would this be acceptable? With some of you it would be fine. With others, I'd probably get my lights knocked out!

Nope. I need to treat you the way you want to be treated. This is what Tony Alessandra, Ph.D. and Michael J. O'Conner, Ph.D. say in their book *The Platinum Rule*. "Do unto others as they'd like done unto them."

What should I do? Well, I KNOW that in the U.S., it's acceptable to offer someone a handshake as a greeting. Until I've gotten to know you better, this is what I need to do. However, once I get to know you, if I believe that you would prefer a hug, then a hug is the most respectful greeting I can give you. In fact, with some people in my life, a handshake would be inappropriate. If I went up to my grandmother and gave her a handshake, she'd be wondering what was wrong. If I walked into the office of one of my clients in North Carolina and didn't give my good friend Shirley a hug as she greets me at the door, I'd be in trouble!

Becoming an expert communicator

So, how do I find out how someone else wants to be treated? I've got to get to know him or her. This leads us to the second characteristic of the energizer – becoming an expert communicator.

The more you communicate with folks, the more you'll get to know them. The biggest key to being a great communicator is learning how to listen. Since this is not a chapter on communication skills, I'll skip the basics of listening and get to the issue that affects your ability to energize others – paying attention.

Paying Attention

I realize that this seems obvious, but is it? I had a supervisor once who was proud of his ability to "multi-task." You'd walk into his office and share an issue with him, the entire time staring at his back. If you can't give 100% of your attention to the employee, I can guarantee that you'll kill their energy. I'm pretty convinced that this manager was actually listening every time I spoke with him in his office – he was quite good at doing three or four things at once. And yet I still would walk out of his office with less energy than when I'd entered. Even the appearance of attention and respect will energize someone.

Active Listening

How do you make sure the other person knows you're there? Use a very simple technique called "active listening." Throughout the conversation, use eye contact and facial expressions to indicate understanding of the message. Frequently summarize what you're hearing and ask questions that show that you are interested in the conversation. Active listening is such a simple skill that creates a great deal of energy during any dialogue.

Giving Recognition and Complements

Energizers are experts at giving recognition and complements. They are quick to notice when someone does something positive. Ken Blanchard, PhD, author of the One Minute Manager series, talks about "catching people doing something right."

In our lives, there is a tendency to be critical of others. Much of the same energy is required to notice positive things and comment on them.

During a class on performance appraisals, I actually had a manager tell me that she didn't see the need to complement someone on work that they're supposed to be doing well anyway. In fact, this is the best time to notice and remark.

I am not saying that when people do exceptional work, it shouldn't be recognized. But it's often the everyday worker who NEVER hears positive comments about her work. This can be very de-motivating.

Start by actively noticing what is going on around you. When you notice someone doing something that is beneficial to the organization, let him know that you noticed. He'll walk away feeling a bit more energy than before. By the way, even your supervisor can be complemented without fear of "brown-nosing." Just tell her that you appreciate the time she put in assisting you with your last project. This is a very powerful practice that takes very little time and energy but yields a great deal of benefit.

How do you receive complements?

By the way, receiving complements appropriately is another sign of an energizer. When you receive recognition or a complement, what do you say? If it's anything other than thank you, you've responded inappropriately. A complement is a gift. If you respond by putting yourself down, you've just rejected the gift.

For example, after a speech recently, I went up to one of my speaker buddies to tell her what an excellent job she'd done. She said that it wasn't bad but that she'd messed up on a couple of things.

This is what I call "yes, butting." She agreed with the complement but then added her "But I could have done better" caveat. Instead of accepting my complement, she rejected it.

There are two problems here. First of all, she is killing the ego-boosting remark from me that is beneficial to her self-esteem. But more importantly, she's inadvertently discouraging me from complementing her again.

Simple rule – when someone offers you a complement, accept it with a simple "thank you." Whether you agree with it or not, the individual has a right to have noticed this trait or accomplishment and you need to acknowledge that.

Surprise Energizers

Recognition and complements work best when they're unexpected. That's why I recommend having some SURPRISE in your worklife.

Many managers tell their people that they hate surprises. This is a good managerial philosophy. But one of the things that energizers do beautifully is to occasionally throw in some positive surprises.

There is something very exciting about getting a thank you note when it was not expected. Surprise recognition is great.

There are all kinds of surprises that tend to energize beautifully. Once in a while, take someone out to lunch. At the weekly staff meeting, have bagels and donuts waiting for them when they walk in the room. If you already do this, make it omelettes instead! Doing something that's unexpected and positive gets people excited.

On the TV show Survivor, the final contestants were on a South Pacific Island for over a month. They had "reward challenges" every few days. One of the prizes was a night on a yacht with food and a hot shower. Not only was this exciting, but the big surprise was that Sean, the winner of this challenge, after arriving on the ship, discovered that the producers had flown in a special guest to act as the captain – his father! You could see the energy come into his body and rejuvenate him. The next morning, care packages arrived for the other five contestants! Missing their families, it was heartwarming to watch them open their packages and read letters from home and snack on some of their favorite comfort foods.

I am known within my family as someone who loves surprises. Years ago my brother, Joe and my nephew, Jack had flown to Florida to visit my parents and grandmothers. On that Friday, I was at work discussing with my close friend Mimi that I was a little bummed because my mom was having a family gathering on Saturday in Jack's honor. She said I ought to just go! So I grabbed a flight certificate I'd had from being bumped once and took the first plane out on Saturday morning. A few hours later, I hopped out of my rental car and walked in the door of my folk's condo. Not only did I get to be a part of the festivities, but the entire party was energized by my little surprise.

I like to have some surprises in my training classes as well. I know that if my students expect some fun but don't know exactly what's coming next, they'll stay alert throughout the program. I'll often give out prizes for participation, team activities and even being back from breaks on time. But because they never know when a prize is coming, they are energized throughout the day to pay attention and participate in the learning process.

The Real "You"

Being respectful is critical. Listening actively makes folks feel that you care. Giving complements and recognition motivates employees to work even harder. And surprises are a fun way to get people excited. But the accomplished energizer knows that none of it works unless you are willing to be real. You've got to be sincere and authentic. When people see that you are exactly who you claim to be, they are energized to be around you.

Earlier, I gave you an example of the platinum rule by saying that I like to hug people but should only hug folks if that's their preference. Some of you were probably reading that and thinking, "You mean if the other person prefers a hug as a greeting, I've got to hug her? What if I don't LIKE to hug people?" The simple answer is, don't hug! You've got to be yourself. One of my closest friends, whom I trust implicitly is also a woman who is just not a hugger. Should she feel obligated to hug me since that's the way I want to be treated? Not at all. It wouldn't be genuine.

Respect comes from being sincere in all that you say and do. Some people energize others through their honesty. Others do it through their passion. Some energize by organizing people and events around them. Others do so by finding the fun in everything that happens in life.

My very first paid speaking opportunity came when I was working as a college administrator. I was asked to come to Syracuse University to keynote a student "community development" program. Although the speech went very well, it was not anything like the speeches I give today. The big difference was in the examples. The Syracuse speech had quotes from famous people and stories from books such as Robert Fulgham's "All I Really Need to Know I Learned in Kindergarten." After joining the National Speakers Association and attending workshops and conventions, I learned that your speeches should be filled with personal stories.

Today, my speeches include a great deal of anecdotes about students I've had, friends, family and other aspects of my life which help to tell the audience about me and who I am. These stories cement my points very effectively. The more I share of my true self, the more I can energize people to make a difference in their own lives.

Find Your Own Way

There's no one correct way to energize people. The most critical aspect is to be authentic in all of your interactions. When a person believes you're being true to yourself, she feels more comfortable being around you. It is then so much easier to use all of the other techniques and qualities discussed in this chapter. The more you can show folks that you enjoy your life, the more they feel excited to enjoy theirs. Energy is an important aspect of the workplace. The more you can energize people, the more they'll enjoy their work and therefore be more successful.

Harvesting Your Full Potential in the 21st Century

How to tap into the natural creativity and talents that lie dormant within your people.

Mark J. Sadlek

Mark Sadlek's belief in the absolute talents and creative gifts that lie within each individual has guided thousands onto a life path which is positive, authentic, and personally rewarding. Individuals as well as organizations, from management to sales teams, all benefit from Mark's messages that encourage creative performance improvements.

Inspiring his presentations, Mark's background includes sales, training and leadership roles in both the corporate and non-profit industries. His speaking style is rich with stories that frequently touch the fabric of the soul.

Inspirational Keynote Speeches:
- Harvest: Reaping Your Life's Purpose,
  Achieving Life Success

- Plant Your Seed:
  The Power of 21st Century Leadership

- A Penny for Your Thought:
  3-Steps to Capture Your Creativity

- The Light is Green:
  Facing the Intersections in Your Life

Harvest Seminars & Consulting
Dallas, TX • (866) 941-5698 • www.HarvestSeminars.com

Mark J. Sadlek

Harvesting Your Full Potential in the 21st Century

How to tap into the natural creativity and talents that lie dormant within your people.

Do you ever wonder where America's next wave of performance and productivity enhancement will come from?

Think about it. First there was the Agricultural Age, where mankind's primary focus was on the efficient production and distribution of necessary farm products to support the local communities. Whole communities based their productivity and prosperity on the natural gifts of the land. When the farmer nurtured those natural gifts the harvest was prosperous, and the surrounding community shared in the riches of its purpose.

Next came the Industrial Revolution in which mankind saw the mass production and quality duplication of products; everything from pencils, to refrigerators, to cars, all the way up to the massive, heavy duty equipment utilized in factories and on farms today. The Industrial Revolution brought on a prosperity that extended beyond the natural gifts of the land. Whole cities and towns flourished based on the newfound productivity and prosperity that came with the jobs tied to the assembly line. This began the shift. Suddenly, the performance and productivity of men and women were based more on the equipment they utilized than on their own natural creativity and talents.

It wasn't until the later part of the 20th Century when the next level of productivity and performance improvements were realized brought on by the Technological & Communication Era. The conversion was rapid by historical standards. America was no longer beholden to the perceived limited output measured by physical mass production and shear quantity. Utilizing technological and advanced communication devices, a level of speed and productivity was discovered that is, and remains unmatched. Once again, productivity improvement was found outside the realm of the individual. This time the quantum leaps were inspired by the utilization of devices, which manifested an ever-increasing level of performance based on speed and the transfer of information.

In all these ages, revolutions and eras of productivity improvements, one important element was left out...the individual. With every step forward in productivity, less and less reliance was placed on the individual performing the work. They became robotic performers of newly devised functions. Performing the duties, but in the majority of cases, the individual was not to stray from the calculated functions. In other words, don't be creative.

Now, to be sure, there were a good number of cases in which individuals within an organization used their own creativity. Mankind and our economy would not have made the strides that were made in the industrial and technological ages, were it not for individual creativity. However, that was primarily limited to a small percentage of individuals who created the new ideas and tools. At that point, the masses need only simply show up and perform the required functions.

That brings us back to our original question. Where will the next wave of performance and productivity improvement come from? I believe the answer lies in the Philosophy of the Harvest; tapping into the natural creativity and talents that lie dormant within each individual who makes up your team. Just like the farmer who's prosperity was based on the natural gifts of the land, so too can your organization's next level of performance improvement, and long-term prosperity be based on nurturing the natural gifts and talents that lie within each and every one of your employees.

Integrate the creativity and natural talents of each individual with the productivity enhancements from the technological and industrial eras, and I believe we will experience quantum leaps in creativity and performance improvements that are considered unfathomable at this time. This chapter offers a roadmap on how to harvest your employees' and organization's fullest potential, thereby achieving the next wave of performance and productivity enhancements in the 21st Century.

Harvesting - 21st Century Style

So how do you unearth, nurture and reap the natural creative talents that lie within each individual? It will require an unprecedented focus and approach to the development of the individual. As stated earlier, historical organizational development has focused on the improvement of processes, with individuals merely supporting those processes. In the 21st century, corporations, managers, leaders and employees at all levels will do well to reverse that focus. In its place, the focus should be on how to develop the creativity and natural talents of the employee, which in turn can then be supported by the superior processes that have already been developed. By doing so, the level of new products, services and other quality of life amenities will reach explosive levels never before imagined.

The Harvest Process has multiple layers to it. For purposes of this book, I will focus on three distinct approaches for harvesting your organization's full potential in the 21st century. The first approach offers insights for a more traditional "old-school" style management company; the second for a progressive, "new-economy" style management organization, and the third approach is for individual employees in general, no matter what type of organization he or she belongs to.

Harvesting in "Scorched Earth"

A good number of companies continue to base their overriding management style on the roles and behaviors they utilized during their successful years, some dating back to the early and mid-twentieth century. These companies tend to be from more traditional industries, those rooted in the pre-Technological & Communication Era. Starting in the 1980's, many of these companies were downsized, acquired, gutted and pretty much left for "scorched earth". The feeling on the inside is that nothing will grow there. Ironically, even though many of these companies still face ever-increasing challenges in today's marketplace, it is difficult for their management to consider any type of leadership change that is counter to the methods or philosophies they utilized during their glory years. To attempt a bold new approach that focuses on the internal development of individual creativity and initiative, more than likely is so contrary to the corporate beliefs that such an approach is doomed for rejection or could cause more harm than good. Quite frankly, the leadership is probably not ready to assimilate that style and philosophy, and therefore, not likely to support their employees on this new path, even if they were convinced to implement it. The results could very well be further chaos, employee dissension and loss of revenue.

The Harvest belief states there is life and creativity in these so-called "scorched earth" companies. We merely need to prep the soil in such a way that allows the seeds of individual creativity to be sown. The Harvest approach implements programs that appeal to the traditional management philosophies, but at the same time nurtures the creative development of individual employees. Experience shows that one of the most successful programs focuses on the development of group presentation and/or public speaking skills. The success however, lies in how the program is implemented. The traditional classroom style, stand and lecture program format will not achieve the desired results. What is important is that each participant has multiple opportunities to actively hone his or her skills and self-confidence in a peer group setting. The most effective programs offer immediate, intuitive coaching that emphasizes both support for individual successes, as well as the appropriate amount of personalized encouragement. This approach ultimately pushes the employee to even higher levels of confidence, and ultimately "out-of-the-box" creative thinking and personal initiative; characteristics that are vital to individual as well as organizational growth.

Whether it is a sales team, an engineering group or a customer service staff, this approach works! Its safe topic makes it acceptable to even the most traditional management styles. More importantly, the workshop allows the individual participants to develop skills outside their normal functions, thereby offering a safe environment in which to learn and grow.

In the late 1990's, this very approach succeeded beautifully with a major international company in the construction materials industry. Having enjoyed exponential sales growth in the 80's, the company's management soon became lax in its support of its independent distributor sales representatives. As the over-all industry became aggressively competitive in the early 90's, the company's typical representative actually performed fewer and fewer pro-active selling activities, mostly due to lack of training and support from the manufacturer. What resulted was nearly disastrous; prices fell, margins shrunk, and the morale of the representatives shriveled. Faced with this dilemma, the company's President approved a safe, but novel program I developed for its representatives. It was billed as a sales presentation skill development program, and was offered at locations around the country. What transpired was nothing short of amazing! At the start of each session the reps walked in with lowered heads, poor morale, and questioning why the program was needed. Without fail, after three days of interactive work by the participants, each representative departed the training program with heightened self-confidence in their own abilities, and a personal willingness to initiate action plans to achieve greater sales results. Did the program work? Absolutely! Company records showed a ten-fold increase in the level of pro-active sales activity initiated by its independent distributor network.

The Harvest approach nurtured the "scorched earth" by providing a program that easily fit the philosophies of the current leadership, however, the implementation of the program succeeded in unearthing the creative talents and dedications of their people in the field.

Harvesting in "Fertile Ground"

The Harvest approach for companies that have thrived in the new economy is considerably different than those in the "scorched earth" scenario. These companies tend to be much more forward thinking in their leadership approach to individual creativity and participatory management. This style of organization thrives in "fertile ground". Growth typically has come fast for them. Often times however, they can be challenged by too wild a growth, which if not properly tended can become overrun and ultimately make them prone to suffocating the organization's overall stability and future growth potential.

It is my experience that leaders, who typically guide organizations operating in "fertile ground", also support the development of individual creativity and personal initiative. These leaders can be successfully approached with programs that deal specifically in the arena of creativity, personal initiative and participatory management. One of my personal favorites is a program that combines an employee behavioral profiling system with an experiential learning challenge course. These type of guided programs assist in creating awareness of individual behavioral strengths and creativity, as well as both personal and organizational growth opportunities. Once this awareness is created, participants are professionally guided, either individually or as a team, to explore the evolution and development of their roles and natural talents, with a specific eye on achieving organizational performance improvement. Think of it as a controlled creative growth, with a clear direction being placed on the talents of the employee specifically linked with the corporate goals and objectives.

Recently, I successfully implemented a similar Harvest program with an exciting upstart Internet-based company in Dallas. When I first met the company they were on a fast track with no shortage of energy, talent or ideas. To his credit, its President, recognized that although their corporate leadership model encouraged personal initiative, a guiding direction was needed to keep all his employees individually challenged, personally satisfied and successful focused on the company objectives. Just as important, he recognized the value of his team continuing to operate at their peak personal creative levels. The Harvest program implemented achieved his stated objectives, and in his words was "the perfect tool to enhance our team structure and empower the employees with confidence in themselves and the team's goals".

The Harvest approach nurtured the "fertile ground" that existed by providing a program that easily fit the philosophies of the leadership. More importantly, its implementation succeeded in nurturing and honing the creative talents of all the employees, thereby helping to keep them in sync with the corporate objectives.

Sowing Your Own Harvest

Whether you work for a "scorched earth" or "fertile ground" style of company, or as an entrepreneur or work at home parent, every individual needs to take steps to "sow your own Harvest". I did that very thing several years ago, which ultimately led me to start Harvest Seminars & Consulting. So how then can you take steps to "sow your own Harvest"? There are multiple steps in the process, however, for purposes of this book, I am going to focus on one of the most critical first steps in the process, personal creative journaling.

Now, more than at any time in our modern history, our lives have become so busy with "things to do" that we allow ourselves little or no time for the development of personal expression. From the moment we wake up to the moment we go to bed, our lives are filled with non-stop noise, activities, responsibilities and distractions; some we control, some we don't. The Harvest approach calls for a controlled, daily free-flow journaling session. The session should last 15-20 minutes, and preferably be held in the morning before you start your day. This allows you the benefit of incorporating your creativity into your daily work or personal activities, thereby positively impacting your career and life direction. If a morning session is not possible, it should then be performed immediately before going to sleep, thus allowing your subconscious the benefit of processing your creative work while you sleep. The free-flow journaling process itself allows you to slow down, re-focus and tap into naturally creative seeds. You will be amazed at what creativity lies dormant within you. Some of your most creative and useful productive ideas will come out of these sessions.

Many types of journaling programs will work, the key is finding one you enjoy, connect with and stay with.

Looking to the Future

Are there productivity and performance improvements that can overtake those achieved from the Industrial and Technology Eras? I have no doubt, and the answer lies within the Philosophy of the Harvest. Whether you work for or lead a corporation, or manage a household, each of us can unearth, nurture and reap our individual creative talents. The 21st Century is ripe for merging the creative talents of each individual with the tremendous process improvements achieved in the previous century. The results of which will be the harvesting of a prosperity and productivity unmatched by even today's standards. Our future lies within the Philosophy of the Harvest. Just like the earlier farmer and community that prospered when they focused on the natural gifts of the land, as each individual prospers, so too will the organizations and communities in which they are affiliated in the 21st Century.

One Scoop or Two: It's Your Attitude! It's Your Choice!

How to gain control of performance and productivity by gaining control of your attitude.

Pauline Shirley

Pauline Shirley, a dynamic, charismatic presenter, speaks from rich experiences in leadership and management. She leads by example. Her insight in today's corporate world makes her shared experiences timely and effective.

Renowned as a uniquely effective communications and leadership expert and mentor for today's culturally diverse workplace, she has presented hundreds of seminars and speeches to audience across the United States, Canada, and Mexico.

Pauline has been a guest on radio and television programs, and is cited in newspapers and magazins such as The Chicago Tribune, Success, Ladies Home Journal, The Washingtonian, and Cosmopolitan.

Pauline Shirley, founder of Executive Solutions Unlimited, served as International President of Toastmasters International in 1994-95. She is also a member of the National Speakers Association, the National Speakers Association of North Texas, and the American Society for Training and Development.

Executive Solutions Unlimited
Richardson, TX • (972) 644-6430 • www.paulineshirley.com

<u>Pauline Shirley</u>

One Scoop or Two: It's Your Attitude! It's Your Choice!

How to gain control of performance and productivity by gaining control of your attitude.

> *It is your attitude. Only you can control it.*
>   *You and you alone determine your attitude.*
> *You cannot control the traffic.*
>   *You can control how you let traffic affect you.*
> *You cannot control the people with whom you work*
>   *You can control how you interact with them.*
> *You cannot control your boss.*
>   *You can control how you react to your boss's management style.*
> *You cannot control the weather.*
>   *You can control how you feel about the weather.*

Attitude Quotient

Researchers tell us that we have 40,000 thoughts a day – with 80% of them negative! Imagine 32,000 negative thoughts in every 24 hours. Your mind can only hold one thought at a time. You can make that one thought positive. Negative thoughts are of no benefit to you. Concentrate on making all your thoughts positive.

What is your attitude quotient? What do you want it to be?

Rate your attitude. On a scale of one to ten, ten being the most positive of attitudes and one being the most negative, where do you rate yourself? Look at yourself from the most objective perspective. Be brave. Be extremely honest with yourself.

<u>Negative 1 2 3 4 5 6 7 8 9 10 Positive</u>

Did you give yourself a six, or maybe an eight? In the future, never settle for less than a ten.

How would your co-workers, employees, boss, friends, clients and family members rate you? Would they all rate you the same? Would there be a wide disparity between how you rate yourself and how others rate you?

Your Most Valuable Asset

"Attitudes are much more important
than aptitudes." – Anonymous

What effect does attitude have on your success?

The Carnegie Institute of Technology test of 10,000 people determined that success is 15% technical and 85% personality factors and being able to deal with other people. Personality factors and being able to deal with other people sharply defined is "attitude." Your attitude determines your success. And what about the success of a company? Companies are comprised of people. The correlation is direct.

Daily we are affected by the attitude of others. We do business with people based on their attitude. We select doctors, hairdressers, dry cleaners, lawyers, accountants, employees and friends, not randomly, but because of their attitude.

Diagnosed with cataracts when I was very young, I wanted to have confidence and faith in my doctor. I sought opinions from three before I selected one. Attitude was the deciding factor. The ophthalmologist of choice is a whistler. He whistles in his office. He whistles when he is preparing for surgery. He whistles while he works. The melodies may be vague, but they are endearing. More importantly, they build confidence. His whistling would not get him into Carnegie Hall or any entertainment gig for that matter. But there is something warmly reassuring about listening to confident whistling prior to surgery. Four times he performed surgery on my eyes and each time his surgical skills progressed. His whistling didn't improve any. It didn't have too. My confidence in him grew, because of his whistling, because of his self-confidence, because of his great attitude.

What effect does your positive attitude have on you?

- A positive attitude builds energy and enthusiasm.
- Being positive opens your mind to creativity.
- A positive attitude is contagious.
- A positive attitude attracts positive events and people.
- A positive attitude makes you look and feel better.

How does your positive attitude influence those around you?

- Your own attitude definitely affects those with whom you come in contact.
- Your positive attitude is transmitted to others.
- People like to associate with people who are optimistic and positive.
- People are influenced to perform well by your positive attitude.
- In most areas of our lives the right attitude is more valuable than skills or talent.

The Capacity to Change

"The greatest revolution of our generation is the discovery that human beings, by changing the inner attitudes of their minds, can change the outer aspects of their lives." – William James

Attitude is how we act, talk, react and interact with others. Attitude is also how we see ourselves. How many times have you heard someone say, "This is the way I am, take it or leave it." When they could be thinking, "I can improve, I can be a better manager, supervisor, leader, co-worker, if I am willing to change my attitude," or, "if I am willing to adjust my style to get along better with others, I will be happier and more satisfied with myself."

It takes twenty-one days to change. For three weeks practice smiling, singing, whistling, and/or positive communications. Look closely at how you communicate. Make conscious decisions and efforts to speak with an optimistic approach. Select and use positive words, phrases, and then whole statements. Incorporate them into your subconscious for daily use.

Positive words communicate a positive attitude.

Use Positive Words	Instead of Negative Words
Can	Can't
Will	Won't
Interesting	Absurd
Good	Bad
Possible	Impossible
Capable	Incompetent
Right	Wrong
Challenging	Unworkable

Choose to use positive phrases	Rather than negative ones.
I will...	Yeah, but
This is important...	I can't believe this...
Thank you.	You're wrong
I appreciate your work	Are you out of your mind?
Let me make some notes...	Won't work
I will check into this now....	Wouldn't work
Let me summarize	You should have
So the problem is...	Not my responsibility
Here is a possibility...	We've tried that. It didn't work.
There is an alternative...	Not my job...

Practice positive statements rather than negative ones.

Compare the first choice with the second in each of the four sets of sentences below. Notice the difference? Read them out loud. Feel the impact of the positive statements.

I will be glad to do that. I will do it first thing tomorrow.
    I'm too busy to do that now. It will have to wait until tomorrow.
That is my first priority, just as soon as I finish these projects.
    I can't do that now. I have too many other things to do.
What do you want to talk about?
    What's your problem?
What happened with that issue?
    I have a problem with the way you did that.

Your Attitude IS Showing

"The outward expression on our face bears the
hidden truths of our heart." – Anonymous

Your attitude shows in everything you do. From a shrug of your shoulders to an edge in your voice, your attitude is obvious.

No one really wants to be in the hospital. Just imagine you are three days post op and have fought a battle with who knows what, the doctors surely don't. It is three o'clock in the afternoon, time for the changing of the medical guard. The new charge nurse slouches into your room and that small glimmer of hope you were tenaciously holding on to blips off your screen Not once in this person's life has a smile ever crossed that face. No laugh lines sully the complexion. And the walk is one of a person who wants to be no place, much less on duty in a hospital and responsible for the health and well being of miscellaneous ill patients. More accurately described, here is someone with a 'baditude' - a really bad case of "attitude." As this nurse walks in, your confidence flees. Your blood pressure goes up, and your much-needed confidence that you will get better drops just as fast. Attitude makes a big difference.

We reflect our internal attitude in our external actions. Gestures, facial expressions and body language deliver messages more graphic than words. Be fully cognizant of the messages you are sending without even opening your mouth. The following are examples of attitude messages delivered through hand gestures, posture, body language and facial expressions.

Attitude shows in your hands.

Gesture	Message
Open hands, palms up	Suggests honesty and openness
Rubbing hands together	Positive anticipation
Strong handshake	Confidence, friendliness
Pointing, stabbing with hands	Negative message
Making a fist	Controlled anger
Pounding on table or desk	Anger

There is attitude in your posture.

Body Position	Message
Shoulders back	Confidence, positive attitude
Energetic purposeful stride	Enthusiasm, confidence
Shuffling	Uncertainty
Head down, shoulders slumped	Low self esteem

Body language attitude to avoid.

- Looking down
- Rushing to be seated
- Slumping
- Slouching
- Leg movement
- Crossing arms over chest
- Hands in pockets
- Shrugging indifferently

Proven "cause and effect" of facial expressions.

- If you look sad you feel sad.
- If you look angry, you feel angry.
- If you smile with your whole face, you feel happier.
- A smile, both natural and forced, sends a message to the brain to release endorphins that make us feel better and more positive.

Scoops of New Attitude

Sometimes only a change in viewpoint is needed to convert a tiresome duty into an interesting opportunity. – Alberta Flanders

Your attitude is your choice, all of the time. Make adjustments to eliminate getting caught with a negative attitude.

Every year, just like you, I have another birthday. One recent birthday, we were extremely busy preparing a rental house for new tenants. The time available to paint, fix-up and clean was limited. So limited that we had to work on the evening of my birthday. Now, don't get the impression that I pouted.

I'm painting the utility room. My husband is in the opposite end of the house doing some electrical work. The house is very quiet. He takes a break and comes to where I am. Smiling, he says, "We are really getting in some quality time together aren't we?" Without waiting for a response, he returns to his tasks.

My painting continues uninterrupted, swoosh, swoosh, drip, oops. Suddenly a flash of brilliance! I think, "This is my birthday. It doesn't matter which birthday this is, all birthdays should be memorable. This one should be no exception. Will I remember this birthday because I was painting a house! No. That's not memorable enough!"

Then the brilliance really strikes! "Ah. Ha! I know what will make this birthday memorable. I'll do something I have never done before, or I would admit to if I had. I'll go skinny dipping in the backyard pool!" I go to the other end of the house. My husband is engrossed in his work. I clear my throat. It must be the paint fumes. I get his attention. "I want my birthday to be memorable. Before we leave tonight, I'm going skinny dipping." Now I have his full attention. "Are you with me or not?" He smiles. Now, I really do have his attention!

Lacking flashes of brilliance, simple exercises also adjust your attitude. Try these.

Attitude Adjustment Number One:
Feeling negative and down in the dumps?

Take a moment, right now. Stand up. Assume the position of being down in the dumps. Slump your shoulders. Let your head hang down and look down at the floor. Move your feet restlessly. How do you feel? Are the blues settling in? Whoa! Don't let them settle in too much.

Try it another way. This time, stand up straight, the way your mother always admonished you to do. Put your shoulders back. Raise your chin slightly. Place your feet solidly on the floor balancing strongly on both feet. Look forward or look at someone and make friendly eye-to-eye contact. The physiological changes in your posture make you feel better.

Attitude Adjustment Number Two: Lack confidence in doing something or in handling a particular situation?

In your mind's eye, visualize how you wish to handle it. Practice mentally. Include the desired results in your new positive visualization. Repeat this exercise several times a day prior to practical use. Relax. Let the new positive attitude in your subconscious mind take over.

Attitude Adjustment Number Three: Spirits need uplifting?

Simply smile. Smile to yourself. Look in the mirror and smile. Smile at someone. Just smile.

Lifting up of the corners of your mouth to form a smile, whether real or forced, sends a message to your brain. Upon receiving the message, your brain releases endorphins. Endorphins make you feel better – naturally.

You have total control over our own attitude. You may choose to be negative and look at the world around us through grungy, negative glasses, or you may opt to function with an attitude of relentless optimism. It is your choice.

Daily you are affected by the attitude of others. Daily your attitude influences people around you. Your attitude is your decision. One scoop or two? Positive or negative? You decide.

> *"There is little difference in people,*
> *but that little difference makes a big difference.*
> *The little difference is attitude.*
> *The big difference is whether it is positive or negative."*
> *– Clement Stone*

CHAPTER THIRTEEN

Make Peace - Make Money

Peacemaking in the Workplace.

Linda Byars Swindling, J.D.

A consultant and professional speaker, Linda Byars Swindling helps managers, business owners and professionals increase their negotiation skills while avoiding legal disputes. She is a sought-after attorney-mediator who helps judges resolve cases on their dockets and serves Of Counsel to a Texas law firm.

Linda is co-author of *The Consultant's Legal Guide*, and is creator of Peacemaker Productions which offers multimedia training programs:

- Managing Without Hassle
- Hiring and Firing the Legal Way
- Workplace Violence
- Employee Retainment: Keeping Your Key People
- Managing Your Manager: Negotiating With Your Boss

Trained by the Attorney-Mediators Institute and the Program on Negotiations at Harvard Law School, Linda is a frequent presenter for the Dallas Convention & Visitors Bureau, ASTD, Arthur Andersen, and Meeting Professionals International. This member of the National Speakers Association leaves her audiences laughing in the aisles and out of the courthouse.

Linda Byars Swindling
Carrollton, TX • (972) 416-3652 • www.lindaswindling.com

Linda Byars Swindling

Make Peace - Make Money

Peacemaking in the Workplace.

You have heard how motivation, communication, stress reduction and time management can increase your employees' productivity . You would love to give your employees the proper incentives and use some of the supervisory skills you have learned. You are eager to try all of these management techniques if you can just figure out how to do one thing: stop the infighting and ongoing conflict.

Conflict at Work

Unresolved conflict can dramatically decrease productivity and performance in the workplace. It can result in employee complaints to governmental agencies and even litigation. What is frustrating is that many matters could have been resolved or even avoided completely. For example, consider the following situation:

Scenario: The Jokes Are Not Funny

Imagine that you find out that KarenAnne, one of your direct reports, filed a complaint with the company's human resources department. Apparently, a co-worker has been sending her email correspondence with what she considers inappropriate humor. KarenAnne doesn't appreciate the sexual innuendo, and she has threatened to file a hostile workplace sexual harassment claim with the Equal Employment Opportunity Commission (EEOC). You know that her claim may also lead to litigation.

When KarenAnne is asked if she spoke to her co-worker regarding the emails, she said "No, because I knew it wouldn't do any good. I would just have been considered a 'prude' and stirring up trouble." Unfortunately, you know she is probably right. The group is tight and quick to stand up for each other. You also know that her co-workers treat anyone with a different opinion as an outsider.

You are frustrated that you are just now being informed about KarenAnne's feelings and these emails. You wonder if her silence for so long led her co-workers to believe she welcomed the jokes. In addition, you wonder if anyone else feels uncomfortable and is just not speaking up. What do you do now?

Commentary

Most employees file government complaints and lawsuits because they believe they were not listened to or were treated unfairly. They may feel a lack of respect or that they had no power over their work conditions.

Even if KarenAnne's complaint is resolved satisfactory, you have a continuing problem that involves making everyone feel comfortable in the workplace; comfortable to voice concerns to you and comfortable to tell a co-worker that behavior is not welcomed. You probably cannot eliminate all complaints, but you can substantially reduce them.

Stress/Success Approach

One immediate thing you can do is to apply the "stress/success" approach. You can make it a policy that it is every employee's job to decrease stress and increase success. All employees' actions should focus on increasing success. While some actions to achieve success might increase stress to accomplish the goal, never should the action increase stress and detract from the success of the company. Unprofessional emails or actions that make others feel isolated add to that individual's stress and decrease from the company's success. Therefore, unprofessional behavior is not allowed. This fairly simple approach can help employees guide themselves through those situations that many of us dismiss as common sense. It also shows your employees that you are committed to their personal success.

Scenario: Jose's "Vacation"

Suppose co-workers are aggravated with the time Jose has been away from work. They spend time talking about how he does not pull his weight and is a slacker. Jose is left out of important conversations. His co-workers secretly hope they can make him look bad and so uninformed that Jose is reprimanded or dismissed. You know Jose's co-workers are spending far more time worrying about Jose than the time Jose is actually missing from work.

You also know that Jose is on a strict medical regimen and misses work for kidney dialysis. Jose has asked you not to say anything about his treatment. He has told you that he is waiting for a kidney transplant. With his age and the shortage of donors, he tells you that he doesn't want to get his hopes up. In addition, Jose is afraid that his co-workers will treat him differently if they find out that he is so ill. You believe that the Americans with Disabilities Act ("ADA") may also come into play. Never have you felt so pulled in so many directions. You wish you could tell everyone to M-Y-O-B ("Mind Your Own Business") and get out of the middle of this situation. You keep wondering why you can't just go to work and not worry about all this personal stuff.

Commentary

So what do you do with the situation involving Jose? Are you forced to tell everyone about Jose's kidney disease? How do you tell those co-workers to MYOB and put an end to the gossip?

One of the best ways may be to call a meeting of all the workers in your department or make an announcement at the end of a regular business meeting. You may want to state the following:

"I am aware that some of you have been discussing how other employees are treated under the attendance policy. If anyone is receiving different treatment, it is because I approved that treatment for good reasons. If you have good reasons to change your attendance, please see me. If not, you are still under the same employment policies that you agreed to when you came to work here. I do not care who has said what up to this meeting. However, from this point forward, if you have a complaint or suggestion about any of our policies, I want you to come see me instead of spending time discussing it without getting the facts. I am always open to suggestions that make our policies better. If you have any ideas, please come see me. Now, let's get back to work."

Look what happened in your conversation. You let your employees know you are aware of the gossip, you want it to stop and you gave them the rules about attendance and enforcement of the policy. You did not reveal the personal reasons behind Jose's special treatment. Neither Jose nor the gossiping employees were identified. Instead, you addressed the gossip in a "from this point forward" conversation. You wiped the slate clean for past gossip and put the employees on notice that no more would be tolerated. Finally, you allow people an outlet other than gossiping to voice their frustration, and you ended on a positive note. You have performed some great peacemaking.

The Peacemaker's Path

Peacemaking is tough. It is critical to stay in control when others are not. To come up with the best peacemaking solutions, it helps to remember the "I TREC" method. The letters "I TREC" stand for the words:
- InTake
- Restate
- Evaluate
- Create

InTake

The "I" in "InTake" stands for the person who controls each of our responses...us or "I." Sometimes we forget that no one forces us to act, but that we choose to react in a certain matter. For some reason, remembering that you are in control of your reactions helps when an employee is out of control. The word "InTake" reminds you not to react before you have all the facts. It is important to gather or "take in" the information you need before acting. Here are some tips to help you do this well.
- Stop your "auto pilot." Stop the knee jerk reaction and breathe instead. Remind yourself that you are not at your best when you are stressed.
- Look at the situation and the "driver" before you respond. Ask yourself, "Is this a normally in-control person who is

overly stressed?" or "Is this a person who has been counseled repeatedly?" or "Is this a person who could turn violent?" Identifying the situation and the person involved will help you determine the correct action. If you have a potentially violent employee, you know that safety is your main concern. If your employee is frustrated, you may need to let him or her vent. If you have someone who has been disciplined on several occasions, you may need to concentrate on the next disciplinary action and proper documentation.

- Listen actively. Make sure you hear what is being said. Many of us initially go into a defensive mode and do not hear what the issue is, or we attempt to address the wrong issue.

Restate

The "R" in I TREC stands for "Restate." Your next step is to concentrate on restating what you just heard. Even though you think you have the facts of an incident, it is important to double-check and verify the information. It is best to restate what you have observed and follow these guidelines:

- Stay Calm. People think better when they are not agitated. Repeat the words or restate the actions you have just experienced back to your employees. Many times, employees will correct you or even apologize once they hear their words or actions repeated.
- Clarify Issues. Make sure you have all the details before you respond to anything. One effective way to do this is to ask to take notes and write down each item that an employee is telling you. Later, you not only have a record of the incident, but you also have an outline on how to address the concerns.
- Ask, Ask and Ask. Make sure you ask questions and determine just exactly what you are responding to before proceeding. Many times just asking questions will let even a distraught employee know you are listening and are attempting to understand.

*E*valuate

Once you are clear on the objective facts, you are ready to determine your next course of action. To evaluate well, make sure you:

- Separate the issues from emotions. Asking the employee to clarify his or her position should help an employee vent and get to the facts. Staying calm will help you determine possible problems instead of seeing an employee's comments as personal attacks.
- Be prepared to postpone. If you need to investigate a situation or if you are too upset to proceed, tell the employee you will meet with him or her later. A couple of suggestions, "Wow, you have put a lot of thought into this. I want to put the same amount of effort in my response." Or "I just did not know this was an issue. I am going to have to look into this so I can respond to your concerns. Let's talk tomorrow at 9 a.m."
- Leave yourself an out. Practice now what you might say if you are caught off guard. You deserve a chance to think things through, and your employees deserve thoughtful responses regarding their concerns.

*C*reate

Only after you have completed the other three steps, are you ready to problem solve. Now you can:

- Generate options. Try to avoid considering just one solution. Be creative. Come up with at least two or three solutions before choosing the best one.
- Remain open to possibilities. Consider options even if they are not the standard way of doing things.
- Collaborate and cooperate. Ask your employees to suggest and provide solutions. Usually, they are the ones who have spent the most time considering the situation and are the ones who will have to live with the solution.

How would you apply the I TREC method to the following scenario?

Scenario: The Cold War

Imagine taking a new product to the market place. In this product launch you have been handed a very tight and almost impossible deadline to meet. At the end of the initial meeting with your team, you know you are in trouble. To say the least, the meeting was a total disaster. The atmosphere was cold, and no one provided any insight. You hand picked the best for this project. However, no one offered any new ideas or volunteered to take responsibility. You left thinking that you did not communicate either with the right words or to the right folks.

Apparently, two of your employees are at war with each other. They have built up factions with co-employees and are pre-occupied with who is talking to whom. This behavior began when one employee was given a promotion another felt he deserved. You never dreamed you would be spending the precious little time you have breaking up petty fights. You can tell that your speech about team-work and co-operation was totally ignored. If you do not stop the unproductive fighting and start working immediately it could delay the product launch and very unpleasant things could happen with your job. What do you do?

Commentary

One of the first things you might do is to call both of the "warring parties" to meet with you. You will ask each what they believe the situation is, and why there is no co-operation. If neither is willing to talk in front of the other, you may have to hold these conversations privately and then reconvene to restate the issues you have ascertained. Be careful to spend the time needed to "InTake" and "Restate" the issues. These two stages will help you get to the real problems instead of just the emotions or hurt feelings involved in the promotion.

Do not forget to leave yourself time to "Evaluate." If you need to take a break to consider options, tell everyone that you will meet the next day or a few hours later. This is extremely helpful if both parties have been emotional. A good night's sleep or time away from a problem, does help resolve matters. As homework, tell everyone they must bring some ideas to resolve this situation when you meet again.

Whether you postpone or directly continue with the "Create"

portion of the conversation, remember that your employees share the responsibility for creating a solution. It is not your job to come up with all the solutions. People tend to support what they create. If your employees participate in solving their problem, they are more likely to support the solution and police the enforcement themselves. This joint problem solving approach is also called interest-based problem solving or the "win-win" approach. Because joint problem solving is collaborative and employees are treated as adults, interest-based problem solving is considered more fair and respectful.

Encourage Individual Dispute Resolution

While the scenarios above reflected a manager's involvement, one way to instill peacemaking is to make it company practice to reward and encourage individual dispute resolution. If the issue is a personal one and your employees are coming to you to "break up the fight", ask them what they have tried to do to resolve the issue. Where appropriate, have your employees try to work out a resolution with each other before involving you. Tell your employees you are here if they cannot work out their differences, but you want them to try to resolve the issue first before seeing you. Of course, exceptions exist if the problem is sexual harassment or discrimination. However, if you want those employees to grow up and act like the adults you desire, you must take yourself out of the referee role.

Conclusion

Peacemaking becomes easier with practice. By modeling the behavior you want, your employees will catch on. Remind them to increase success and decrease stress. Encourage individual dispute resolution. Find the best solutions by InTaking and Restating before you Evaluate and Create. Most of all stay calm, be creative and keep your sense of humor.

CHAPTER FOURTEEN

Stress Is Less – Less Is More... Productivity That Is!

How to create a higher level of commitment in employees by aligning personalities, behaviors, and accomplishments.

Russ Yaquinto

An accomplished Leader and Human Development Specialist with an authentic, yet inspirational style of communication, Russ Yaquinto has more than twenty-five years experience in Human Resources and Organization Development.

Russ is Vice President Consulting Services with Right Management Consultants, a premiere international provider of human resources services. He is also founder and principal of The Change Connection, dedicated to helping people and organizations learn, grow and change.

Russ is past President of the International Association of Career Management Professionals. He is active in the American Society for Training and Development, the International Coaching Federation, and the National Speakers Association.

Key areas of expertise:
- Personal / Professional Success
- Executive Assimilation
- Career Management
- Change Strategies
- Organizational Effectiveness

The Change Connection
Dallas, TX • (972) 239-1700 • email: russy@flash.net

Russ Yaquinto

Stress Is Less – Less Is More...
Productivity That Is!

How to create a higher level of commitment in employees by aligning personalities, behaviors, and accomplishments.

With the mega advancements in technology and the ever changing stage in the drama of the business world, it almost seems secondary for employers to be concerned about the well being of workers. What's the big deal about stress in the workplace? Isn't it a fact of life that each individual needs to deal with? Why all the attention to employee harmony and comfort?

The answer lies in the payoffs of better attitudes toward self, each other, the company and customers. Less stress typically begets better performance and greater productivity. There ultimately is a bottom line impact based on stronger commitments, greater efficiencies, higher outputs and client satisfaction. While employers may not be responsible for all stress and how people manage it, they are well advised to at least be aware of various personality styles and reactions and how these factors may affect behaviors and accomplishments.

DRIVER MENTALITY

Henry, a production manager having a particularly troublesome quarter, commented "If I didn't have to deal so much with people, I could get a lot more work done". He is the stereotypical "driver"; fast moving, decisive, bottom line oriented. Henry's sights are always set on action and results, regardless of others' styles, preferences, priorities or life circumstances. He probably subscribes to Dilbert's Rule of Order, "The more crap you put up with, the more crap you are going to get."

What's with that? How does anyone get off thinking employees are a nuisance? And yet, this conviction was popular with some managers in the 60's and 70's. As computers and automation became more pragmatic and affordable in the 80's and 90's, there was a heightened excitement about the notion of paperless systems and instantaneous updating and sharing of information. This created a monster steamroller of quicker transactions, vast amounts of data to handle, expanded tasks and responsibilities, multi-media processes and generally more forces to reckon with. (Enter...more stress).

Mac Martirossian, Senior Vice President of Howard Schultz and Associates, an international financial services firm, observes, "With the increase in amounts and speed of information, the good news is there is more data available quicker, while the bad news is there is more to absorb, and everyone expects instantaneous attention. This puts tremendous pressure on a given individual to respond almost immediately." He reflects that, "This cuts down on creativity because there is no time for imagination or innovation."

Employers have also shifted away from the practice of rewarding good performance with job security and long tenure. The norm has evolved to "just in time" employment and non-traditional work arrangements based on specific needs and convenience, and with no intention or promise of "permanency". These changes were quite disarming to many folks.

The Henry's of the world may have thought this was not their problem. Well, not so fast Henry! First off, it appears your dream of not needing people is unrealistic, and probably won't be in the foreseeable future. Instead, there is a whole new set of challenges in recruiting and retaining the right people with the right skills, knowledge and motivation for the right job. Otherwise, we have mismatches and resulting friction, which typically shows up in strain, struggle and less than satisfactory performance (and that certainly is your problem).

DESTRUCTIVE

According to B.J. Rone, Co-Founder of Speed Link Communications, Inc., based in the UK, "Stress can take natural abilities and drive, and destroy them. An over stressed individual acts out in uncharacteristic ways. He/she may become irrational, procrastinate, put out sloppy work, miss time, experience more illness, make wrong decisions, just to name a few destructive reactions."

Rone recalls from his consulting days a turnaround situation when a well known and profitable producer of magnetic tape products, was acquired. Among other less sensitive actions, the new owner quickly replaced the company's signage with the name of the parent organization in large letters, while the identity of the acquired company appeared in small, obscure print. The strain generated by this incident, together with other aspects of the transition, was significant and resulted in loss of morale and severely lowered output.

When the business was subsequently acquired by still another company, Rone came into the picture. He closely examined the facility, the organization, and most importantly the climate. The remarkably high stress levels and poor morale were readily apparent, and he arranged some simple steps to rectify the situation. One of the first of several amends was to tear down the then current sign, and throw a party in the parking lot where employees were provided sledge hammers to destroy it. Then a new sign was installed that reinstituted the original company name. The positive impact of management's respectful attitude was phenomenal. Productivity and profitability shot back up to previous industry leading levels.

REMEDIES

Looking on the bright side, employers and their leaders can constructively influence employee performance and productivity by better understanding stress and reactions to it. At the same time, the solution is much more complex than simply resolving to reduce stress levels, then waiting for people to relax and thereby become more efficient. Several issues must be addressed:

Individual Makeup

What are the mental, emotional and psychological orientations of individual employees and work groups? Are the job descriptions and requirements congruent with workers' personal makeup? Some individuals thrive on spontaneity, excitement and loose structure, while others prefer advance planning, tranquility, and clear procedures and rules.

In either case, with congruence comes the makings of job satisfaction, thus less resistance, more willing effort, and even enjoyment. Martirossian observes, "When fun goes out of the job, so does teamwork. You stop communicating, sharing and supporting. Sometimes, the misfit is so pronounced, you become overwhelmed and break down. Then you need extra attention just to get back on track."

Henry would do well to look closer at the specific organizational needs and demands of the jobs and compare them with the people involved. It would also behoove him to be more diligent in his hiring and placement (round pegs in round holes). The closer the match, the less strain and the stronger commitment and output. There are tests, profile instruments and other assessment tools available to help in this effort.

Compatibility

How compatible are the bosses' philosophies and styles with those of their staffs? When we have accord between leaders and their teams, there is a good foundation for mutual respect and trust. Another important aspect of compatibility is harmony among the troops? This does not necessarily mean the parties must have the exact same profiles (i.e. personality, psychological/emotional orientations, etc.). It simply suggests accepting and appreciating people for what they bring to the table.

Compatibility engenders stronger rapport, more cooperation and willingness to work hard for the common good. Henry would have fewer people problems and less stress if he valued his subordinates and peers as a cohesive team of individuals with different contributions to make to the objectives of the business.

Environment

What is the business environment or culture of the company? Does it foster less or more stress? Some organizations are fast-paced, change frequently or place high demands on individuals and teams; if so, they are wise to hire people who like this type of setting (enter ..."Generation Why"). Other employers are more traditional, conservative, preferring stability with slow, steady growth; then they should seek out those who want the less frenetic milieu.

This is another, indeed more fundamental, aspect of compatibility. Perhaps Henry should even check out his own personality and idiosyncrasies as related to the company environment. Where his subordinates are concerned, he may be able to create or influence the environment to more closely align with their preferences.

Leadership Development

What training is provided for managers in leading change and reducing stress? While the so-called "Generation Why" may be more attuned to fast-paced, multi-tasked, quick-changing circumstances, we still have certain personalities that are not comfortable with a steady diet of those things. So, leaders adept at facilitating projects and transitions can expect to reap the benefits of stronger rapport and effective teamwork. Moreover, skills in conflict resolution can be worth their weight in gold.

Henry may require personal help in acknowledging the need for change and diversity, let alone leading the efforts. Once he recognizes the universality of change and it's potential benefits, he can embrace it and help others through it. Developing his skills and acting as a facilitator and resource would undoubtedly get more done than rigid supervision and control.

Non-Traditional Measures

Are there physical or esoteric provisions for employees to help alleviate the undesirable aspects of stress? Some employers provide such things as day care or flexible hours for parents, telecommuting, free meals, exercise facilities, massages in the office, casual dress codes, elaborate break rooms, and "cool work places." Others reach out to recognize individuals and teams for their efforts and accomplishments.

The expenses of these non-traditional perks have resulted in paybacks well worth the initial outlay. Workers tend to enjoy their environments, and feel more relaxed and less stressed, while producing more as a natural outcome of these positive influences. Henry should take a lesson from the famous Hawthorne experiments, where the sheer attention given to employees resulted in improved productivity.

Self-Reliance

To what extent is self-reliance encouraged and supported? The days of "entitlement" are a thing of the past. People are now expected to direct their own careers. In light of this, employers are providing more opportunities for mentoring, and personal and professional development. They encourage individuals to learn, grow and take charge of their destiny.

Allowing time and providing financial support for formal education, workshops, coaching and skill building experiences are part of some companies' portfolios from which individuals can select options to develop their careers. The concept of corporate universities is a good example that has grown in popularity.

While the impetus is on individuals taking responsibility for themselves, the marketplace is relating to workers in more of a partnership role. Meanwhile, we have given up the old model of infinite employment with a single employer. (This can exacerbate stress levels in those people who seek long term security). On the other hand, there are more options available for people to utilize in creating or directing their success (which can be exciting and fulfilling).

GOOD STRESS

Most of us agree that some stress is good; the kind that taps our adrenaline and drives us to meet deadlines or other demands. Common for sales professionals and managers, appropriate amounts of this type of stress is desirable to meet quotas and keep going in the face of adversity. Many of us enjoy the "rush" of a challenging experience when it represents growth, adventure, or potential achievement. Beware that there is usually a threshold beyond which the stress can still become overbearing and counter productive.

DIFFERENT STROKES

In the spirit of accelerated/adult learning principles, business has begun to realize the value of a multi-dimensional approach to employee relations and stress management. It recognizes the assorted ways that people think and behave. There is a heightened appreciation for the notion of "different strokes for different folks". Providing a smorgasbord of opportunities and methodologies, along with a variety of ways to interact with employees, opens the door for reduced tension, enhanced morale and higher productivity.

Bob Bruno, President of B&B Associates, a marketing consulting firm in Dallas, also points out, "There are different categories of stress. We each have some degree of internal (self imposed) tension. This can serve us in beneficial ways when urgency, commitment or closure are important. Or, it can be destructive in terms of confusion, loss of interest, emotional overload or burnout. And there is the external pressure that comes by way of project deadlines, additional responsibilities or duties, irreconcilable differences, or unrealistic expectations."

Bruno admonishes that "Often the price paid for high stress in business is employee terminations, and the costs of turnover can be debilitating. They may include loss of revenue opportunities until a replacement is found, in addition to the expenses of recruiting, hiring and training a new, qualified person, and the costs of that person getting up to speed."

QUESTIONS AND ANSWERS

It is not necessary to ask whether there is stress in the work place...because that's a given. The real issues are: how much, what kind, how severe, and how to deal with it.

As a manager, it is incumbent on you to organize, lead, support and control the workforce as a harmonious team. To help examine the role stress plays in your organization, and how effective you are in your position, here are some basic questions:

- What steps do you take to match individuals' preferences with the work to be done or vice versa?

- How do you select employees who will work well with you and the rest of the team?
- How do you insure that workers are well suited for the organizational environment, including the demands and stress levels to be expected?
- What skills do you have in leading change, and facilitating and channeling stress? Where might you need further development?
- How do you allow for individuals' ownership of their careers while maintaining reasonable control over assignments and getting the job done?

Answers to these questions will reveal a lot about how smooth or bumpy is your ride on the corporate highway. They will also provide a useful map to more effectively navigate the road to top performance and productivity

So...listen up Henry! If people are in your way, and if you believe everyone is on their own when it comes to stress, think again about how work gets done. Look at how success is achieved.

Think about the ways you can make your job easier by making others' easier. As you explore how to reduce and channel stress, remember, less is more!

BOOKS

Corporate Cults: The Insidious Lure of the All-Consuming Organization
by Dave Arnott, published in 2000 by the American Management
Association. ($2.50 shipping and handling ea.) $23.95

ORDERING INFORMATION:
Dave Arnott
Rowlett, Texas
972-475-7164
www.DaveArnott.com

Additional Resources from Tracy Brown

BOOKS

Breaking the Barrier of Bias $14.95

Tracy's Top Tips: Transforming Awareness to Action (1/01) $15.00

AUDIO CASSETTES

The R Word: Succeeding In Spite of Racism $10.00

Breaking the Barrier of Bias (4 Tape Set) $35.00

motiVersity: Motivating While Valuing Diversity (2 Tape Set) $20.00

Maximizing Diversity in Health Care Settings (6 Tape Set) $75.00

ORDERING INFORMATION:

Person To Person Consulting

Tracy Brown

Dallas, Texas

Toll Free: 1-888-316-4447

214-369-2888

www.TracyBrown.com

FREE REPORT

Cultivating Exceptional Employees
This article expands on the chapter featured in *The Productivity Path*, and adds in-depth information and case studies on all four factors essential to cultivating exceptional employees. (FREE on the website at www.coremap.com)

PROFILING TOOL

CORE Multidimensional Awareness Profile
CORE is the premier personality profiling instrument of the new millennium for personal and professional use. CORE measures natural tendencies, preferred functioning modes, personal effectiveness traits, reactionary styles, tolerance levels, and much more. No other profiling instrument provides a more complete personal profile.

BOOKS

Who's Got the Compass? I think I'm lost: A Guide to Finding Your Ideal Self
A bold departure from the typical self-improvement book, Sherry brings together every aspect of the self-discovery process. She hands you a compass that virtually insures you will find your ideal path. This is an essential guide for the most important journey of your lifetime.

ORDERING INFORMATION:

Peak Potentials
Sherry Buffington
Dallas, Texas
Toll Free: 1-877-884-CORE
214-688-1412
www.coremap.com

Additional Resources from Chandler George

AUDIO CASSETTE
How to E-mail Your STRESS to Another Planet ($2.50 S&H) $10.00

PUBLICATIONS
Ageless Energy Manual (68 pages) ($4.50 S&H) $49.00
Energize Your Life (Booklet) (S.A.S.E. w/.55¢ postage) $3.95

SPECIAL PACKAGE
The Ageless Energy Pack (Get all 3!!!) ***FREE Shipping*** $59.95

ORDERING INFORMATION:
Dr. Chandler George
Weatherford, Texas
817-599-0061
www.drgeorgedc.com

AUDIO CASSETTES
Business Builders...Business Busters (JP's most requested keynote presentation)
How to leverage your organization's human capital. (single cassette) $9.95

Customer Service Strategies for the New Millennium
JP Maroney's popular 1/2 day customer service seminar shows how to increase
repeat and referrals sales. (2 cassettes & workbook) $29.95

VIDEO PROGRAMS
Business Builders...Business Busters (JP's most requested keynote presentation)
How to leverage your organization's human capital. (single video) $59.95

Customer Service Strategies for the New Millennium
JP Maroney's popular 1/2 day customer service seminar shows how to increase
repeat and referrals sales. (2 videos & workbook) $99.95

MONTHLY EMPLOYEE DEVELOPMENT SERIES
People Builders: Interactive Audio/Video Learning Series
Receive a new learning module each month featuring a major topic for
improving employee performance and productivity (eg: Customer Service,
Team Building, Communication Skills). Train all of your employees (10, 100, or
1000) for one year subscription at only $129 per month + $5.50 S&H. Each
monthly module includes: video, audio, participant handouts, posters, module feedback form, facilitator success guide, materials storage binder, free
training tips, and more. Call for full details, or visit www.JPMaroney.com/pb

MOTIVATIONAL POSTERS
(Packets of 5 powerful posters JP uses during his presentations)
Is 99.9% Good Enough? (11"x17") $9.95
Business Builders...Business Busters (11"x17") $9.95
Why Customers Don't Return (11"x17") $9.95
12 Customer Service Strategies for the New Millennium (11"x17") $9.95

SPECIAL REPORT
How to Unleash Your Organization's Entrepreneurial Energy
Learn the 3 essential ingredients for creating a corporate culture where
employees think and act like owners and accept personal responsibility for the
organization's success. $19.95

ORDERING INFORMATION:
JP Maroney International
Tyler, Texas
1-800-304-5758
www.JPMaroney.com

Additional Resources from Sarita Maybin

AUDIO CASSETTE

How to Turn Negativity into Possibility...At Work and Beyond!
50 Minute audio program focusing on how to respond to whiners, naysayers and other negativity. Strategies are provided on how to stay positive and keep the contagious effect of negativity from rubbing off on you and your staff.

ORDERING INFORMATION

Sarita Maybin
Oceanside, California
760-758-3155
www.SaritaTalk.com

MANAGING FOR SUCCESS® COLLECTION

MFS Executive Report $75.00

The executive report provides information for any executive to understand their management style and thereby assist them in adapting their behavior to situations.

Internet delivery of report: $85.00

MFS Sales $75.00

Geared specifically towards sales people, this report takes into account the crucial differences between salespeople and other groups of employees. It provides valuable information on ensuring that individuals in sales are placed in the right environment for achieving maximum performance.

Internet delivery of report: $85.00

MFS Employee-Manager $75.00

Our most popular report, this report enables employers and managers to quickly learn how to work more effectively with one-another, to improve communication and working relationships that result in improved performance.

Internet delivery of report: $85.00

Personal Interests and Values $60.00

This instrument measures the relative prominence of six basic interests or motives and helps to reveal hidden motivators that are the driving forces behind individual decisions. A key part of the selection process and critical to identifying best fit for maximizing performance.

Internet delivery of report: $70.00

INTERNET DELIVERY SERVICE (IDS)

All MFS reports may be administered via the internet. To establish your private code and to make final arrangements, call The Price Group at 888-404-0787.

BOOKS

Rejecting Rejections: How To Take Control of Your Life In Uncontrollable Times
A roadmap for understanding the role rejection plays in one's ability to cope with change and powerful principles to regain control and resilience. Based on Price's personal journey from allowing rejection to control her life to a new sense of self-awareness and purpose. (ISBN 0-7872-2681-5, Kendall/Hunt Publishing)

ORDERING INFORMATION:

The Price Group
Addison, Texas
Toll Free: 888-404-0787, 972-404-0787
www.PriceGroupMarketing.com

JOURNALING TOOL

The Harvest Journal: Unearthing Your Seeds for Success
A full calendar year journaling system that links the Philosophy of the Harvest with your own personal roadmap to unearth, nurture and reap the natural creative talents that lie deep within you. Retails at $19.95, ordered through this book offer and SAVE 20% ($16/journal).

AUDIO CASSETTES

Single cassettes retail at $12.50/tape. Order through this book offer and SAVE 20% ($10.00/tape)

Harvest: Reaping Your Life's Purpose, Achieving Life Success
Based on the "Philosophy of the Harvest," this inspirational presentation offers a path for unearthing, nurturing and enhancing your natural, creative talents to achieve vocational success.

Plant Your Seed: The Power of 21st Century Leadership
Do you wonder how our society will surpass the advances achieved in productivity brought on by the Industrial and Technological Ages? This exhilarating presentation offers great promise, and a game plan for both corporate and non-profit organizations.

A Penny For Your Thought: 3-Steps to Capture Your Creativity
Once you experience this dynamic presentation, you'll never view a simple "penny" the same. A 3-step process is used to gain control of your life's direction, and help set a course for more positive, and satisfying future.

The Light Is Green: Facing the Intersections in Your Life
We have all been there at some time in our life...an intersection. Our first thought is the "light is stuck red," not knowing how or which way to move forward. Intersection...dealing with change, some are brought on by corporate mergers, acquisitions, or downsizing; others from personal life changes. This audio presentation is perfect for any group dealing with change.

ORDERING INFORMATION:

Harvest Seminars & Consulting
Dallas, Texas
Toll Free: 1-866-941-5698
214-941-5698
www.HarvestSeminars.com

Audio Cassette
Managing Your Manager: Tips for Negotiating with Your Boss!
These practical tips help you negotiate with the toughest boss and in the most
difficult workplace situation. (50 minutes: Peacemaker Productions) $12.00

VIDEO TAPES
Managing Without the Legal Hassle
Examines reasons employees file complaints and lawsuits, the secrets to avoid-
ing complaints and various employment laws. (approx. 55 minutes-
Peacemaker Productions) $129.00

Hiring & Firing the Legal Way
Learn how to motivate, coach and effectively discipline employees. Hire the
best, prevent discrimination and sexual harassment and terminate legally
when necessary. (approx. 50 minutes-Peacemaker Productions) $129.00

Violence in the Workplace
Handling crisis situations properly can decrease or eliminate confusion and
injury. Guidelines given for identifying potential problems and problem
employees as well as practical safeguards for work and responsibilities under
the law. (approx. 55 minutes-Peacemaker Productions) $129.00

Keeping Your Key People
Learn why great employees leave and how to retain them. Identify key people
and learn the secrets of keeping them. (approx. 25 minutes) $89.00

Book special for entire video series $350.00

BOOK
The Consultant's Legal Guide (Linda Byars Swindling & Elaine Biech)
The only complete, user-friendly overview of legal issues faced by consultants
and business owners. Readers will become comfortable with a wide variety of
contracts and legal language. Includes a diskette in the back of the book con-
taining useful tools, sample forms, checklists, and links to the web.
(Hardbound: Published by Jossey-Bass Pfeiffer ©2000) $50.00

All prices plus shipping & handling of $2.79 per item.

Linda Byars Swindling
Carrollton, Texas
Toll Free 1-877-800-5023
(972) 416-3652
www.lindaswindling.com

**IF YOU WISH TO ORDER ADDITIONAL COPIES OF
THE PRODUCTIVITY PATH, CONTACT:**

Sarita Maybin
Professional Speaker

760.439.8086
FAX 760.439.0277
P.O. Box 2898
Oceanside, CA 92051
email:SARITATALK@aol.com

Helping people work together...better!
www.SaritaTalk.com

*You can also find information on other titles
in The Path Series at www.PathSeries.com*